the Journal

Sober Dating:
Questions for Discussion

CONTENTS

PART III - ARTICLES   47

PART IV – SUMMARY & MEETING RESOURCES 133

Introduction

This book was created to give S.L.A.A. members a format for reading, sharing, and journaling about sober dating. It contains recommendations for reading materials and questions about the readings. S.L.A.A. members have found it useful to follow the meeting format at the end of the book. This format can be followed for a meeting of 2 or of more S.L.A.A. members. We have found that when this format is followed, we are not able to answer all of the questions in each section. This allows the individual to write about what they like and leave the rest. We hope this book will help S.L.A.A. members find and offer support for each other in the sober dating process. This book was not intended to be the authority on dating. It was meant as a springboard for discussion and support. Sober dating may be defined as utilizing the five major resources of the Program while dating (S.L.A.A. Preamble, page 125 of the *S.L.A.A. Basic Text*):

1) **Sobriety.** Our willingness to stop acting out in our own personal bottom-line addictive behavior on a daily basis.
2) **Sponsorship/Meetings.** Our capacity to reach out for the supportive fellowship within S.L.A.A.
3) **Steps.** Our practice of the Twelve Step program of recovery to achieve sexual and emotional sobriety.
4) **Service.** Our giving back to the S.L.A.A. community what we continue to freely receive.
5) **Spirituality.** Our developing a relationship with a Power greater than ourselves which can guide and sustain us in recovery.

Reading materials

The questions in this book encourage reflection on the following readings. Readings included within this book are indicated with an asterisk. *S.L.A.A. Basic Text* is available at https://store.slaafws.org/prod/BO-004.html

- **Romantic Obsession* pamphlet
- "Building Partnerships"
  Chapter 8 from the *S.L.A.A. Basic Text*
- *Journal Focus Booklet: Sober Dating: Articles from the Journal with a focus on sober dating*

Part I – Chapter 8, *S.L.A.A. Basic Text*

Building Partnerships

Read the introduction (first 2 paragraphs of the S.L.A.A. Basic Text page 139).

1. Describe your withdrawal experience.
2. Have you come out of withdrawal? If so, write about what brought you out of it. If not, what is blocking your progress?
3. Do you think it is necessary to come out of withdrawal before you start dating? Write about this.
4. How would coming out of withdrawal before beginning to date be better than dating while still in withdrawal?
5. Are you having new life experiences as a result of your sobriety in S.L.A.A.?
6. Describe any inner experiences of:
   a. personal dignity
   b. self-worth
   c. self-intimacy
   d. intimacy with Higher Power
7. How can these experiences translate into guidelines for exploring partnership?
8. Describe what partnership means to you.

Partnership? Or Living Alone?

Read the S.L.A.A. Basic Text page 139-142.

1. Is the prospect of living alone appealing to you? Write a pros and cons list of living alone.
2. Do you believe that using all the tools of S.L.A.A. recovery (Steps, meetings, service, prayer, and meditation) can give you a healthy relationship? Write about this. Do you feel it should yield a healthy relationship if you do everything "right?" (see question 4 below).
3. Are you just marking time to get healthy enough for your next relationship, even subconsciously? Write about your motives for maintaining sobriety in S.L.A.A.
4. Do you feel entitled to a relationship? Are you resentful towards Higher Power, S.L.A.A. or other people if you haven't found a partnership? Write about any resentments that come up.
5. Write about fears of going back into addiction if you start dating.
6. What takes precedence over the opportunity for romance? For example, do you feel work, meetings or family are more important than romance or dating? Write about this.
7. Is finding a partner the most important thing in your life? Write about this.
8. What are your hobbies and interests? Are you comfortable in solitude?
9. Are you financially independent? Do you look for someone to rescue you financially?
10. Are you able to manage your own emotional needs or feel you need someone to do this for you?

11. Write about the difference between the choice of living alone in sobriety and anorexia.
12. Write about any rewarding friendships and positive life experiences you have found because of your time in S.L.A.A.
13. How do you deal with pain in sobriety?
14. What is authentic love?
15. What gives your life meaning?
16. Is having a steady income, creative outlets, and mutually supportive friendships enough for you or do you crave more? Write about this.
17. Describe addictive relationship(s) you used to try to give yourself a sense of purpose and meaning.
18. Describe relationships where you tried to get rather than give or "rip off" rather than contribute. Copy the following chart. Write your answers in your journal. (examples are in italics):

Person's name and relationship to me	What I tried to get or "rip off" and how I tried to get it	What I could have given or contributed instead
Example: Rob	*Exchanged money (cash, clothing, and jewelry) for sex*	*Could have been in an intimate relationship and shared the "real me"*

19. Page 141. The *S.L.A.A. Basic Text* says, "There could be no enduring meaning in "love" that was a rapid consumption commodity on an open market." Read the following

definitions* and copy the following chart. Write your answers in your journal.

a. Rapid - quickly
b. Consumption - the using up of a resource, an amount of something which is used up.
c. Commodity - a raw material or primary agricultural product that can be bought and sold, such as copper or coffee. Commodities include agricultural products, fuels, and metals and are traded in bulk on a commodity exchange
d. Open market - Anyone can participate in an open market, which is characterized by the absence of tariffs, taxes, licensing requirements, subsidies, unionization, and any other regulations or practices that interfere with naturally functioning operations.

definitions taken from Google dictionary at google.com

Relationships that progressed too quickly	Relationships that consumed too much time and energy	Relationships that had no rule or boundaries

20. Write about the dangers of living alone as described on page 141. How can S.L.A.A. help with this?
21. Write about the benefits of living life in the "spirit of service" page 141.

22. Are there/have there been any non-sexual relationships that are similar to past addictive relationships? (be sure to include causes, heroes, gurus, and yourself). Copy the following chart. Write your answers in your journal.

Person that I have or did have a non-sexual relationship with	Way that it is like past addictive relationships

Partnership in a Committed Relationship

Read the S.L.A.A. Basic Text page 142.

1. According to the reading, what is the difference between a "closed system" and an "open system" in relationships?
   a. List "closed system" relationships that you've had and why you thought they fit the definition of a "closed system" relationship. How did you feel about the relationship? How and why did each end?
      i. Did you commit or think about committing "crimes of passion?" (S.L.A.A. Basic Text, page 144) If so, write about this.
      ii. List fears that were present in the relationship.
   b. List "open system" relationships that you've had and why you thought they fit the definition of an "open system." How did you feel about the relationship? How and why did each end?
      i. Were you open to a "broader range of life experiences?" (*S.L.A.A. Basic Text,* page 145) Write about this.
      ii. List personal freedoms in the relationship.
2. Describe any roles that you played in past relationships:
   a. savior,
   b. jailor
   c. child
   d. deity,
   e. parent.
3. How can S.L.A.A. help us become ready for an "open system" relationship? (*S.L.A.A. Basic Text,* page 146)

9

4. How do you keep your meetings, like the *S.L.A.A. Basic Text* says, "sanctuaries?" (*S.L.A.A. Basic Text*, page 146)

5. Describe instances in addiction when you treated people as objects instead of human beings. Did you feel you had reasons to treat them that way?

6. Did you ever feel wronged and resentful toward your partner (dating or in a relationship) if they unilaterally dropped plans? How does a need for autonomy play a part in this?

The Reconciliation Project

Read the S.L.A.A. Basic Text page 147.

1. Describe the breakdowns in communication that had formerly crippled your relationships.
2. List expectations with reconciliation (yours and theirs, if known) — if you're not reconciling with a partner at the present moment list what you expected in the past.
3. Did you label former partners as sexually inadequate, unspontaneous, constricted, or dull? What does the S.L.A.A. Basic Text say about this?
4. According to the S.L.A.A. Basic Text,
   a. how do you begin to work through old sludge and lay a foundation for cooperation, trust, and intimacy?
   b. how do you deal with?
      i. distrust
      ii. sexual dissatisfaction
      iii. old feelings
      iv. moodiness of your partner
      v. entitlement while reconciling
5. Was sex ever a "form of extortion" (The practice of obtaining something through force or threats.*) for you? Write about this.

*definition taken from Google dictionary at google.com

6. List fears surrounding reconciliation and write a fear inventory on each:
(from conference approved literature: *Step Questions Workbook*)

What's the fear?	Why?	What's my part?	Where have I been selfish?

7. Write about the ideas on communication spelled out on page 151 of the S.L.A.A. Basic Text:
   a. expressing needs ("Yet the very "needs" we were expressing...")
   b. sexual rhythms ("For example, if our partner's sexual rhythm...") — how do you deal with confronting these issues rather than retreating into anorexia?
8. Describe power struggles that you have engaged in with partners.
9. List domestic tasks that you do and tasks that your partner does/did. Is there room for you to do more?
10. What is the benefit if you "stop counting orgasms?"
11. How can this reading (on the Reconciliation Project) help even if you are not considering reconciling with a past partner?
12. How can reconciliation in sobriety be different from your past reconciliations?

New Partnerships

Read the S.L.A.A. Basic Text page 153.

1. List past relationships that you feel you've gotten closure on and don't need to revisit. What helped you see you no longer needed to feel bound by a sense of "unfinished business?"
2. Are there any relationships that you feel need closure or that you have a hope of rekindling some day?
3. Is the urgency to enter a new relationship gone for you? Write about this.
4. List the ways you feel you should live in order to be comfortable and reliably sober.
5. How do you react when you encounter a prospective partner who can't accept you for who you are?
6. What do you do when you develop a crush on someone in a meeting?
7. List relationship possibilities that you chose to avoid.

Potential partner I chose to avoid	Reason

8. Were any myths about another S.L.A.A. member's desirability dispelled after hearing them share in a meeting? If so, write about this.

9. Write about the saying "Let go or be dragged" and how it has applied to past relationships or dating.

10. Do you believe that "the anonymous hand of a higher Power has an influence" (S.L.A.A. Basic Text, page 154) in your finding a partner? Write about what this means to you and your sobriety.

11. Write about the idea that if a partnership was meant to be there's nothing you can do to mess it up; but if it wasn't meant to be there's nothing you can do to fix it. Do you believe this?

12. List relationships in the past where you "tried to build a relationship on novelty." What did each of these relationships teach you?

13. Write about relationships that you've had for a: season, a reason, or a lifetime. Copy the following chart. Write your answers in your journal.

Relationship for a season: Name of person	Reason it's only for a season	Good points of relationship	Bad points of relationship
Example: Tom	I needed someone to help me get over a loss, but he wasn't capable of commitment	He was sympathetic to my grief over the loss	He didn't want an exclusive relationship

Relationship for a reason: Name of person	Reason	Good points of relationship	Bad points of relationship
Example: Andy	I realized that I was a sex and love addict	passionate	He was married

Relationship for a lifetime: Name of person	How I know it will probably last a lifetime	Good points of relationship	Bad points of relationship
Example: Dee	She's been my friend since elementary school	We can talk about anything	She lives far away – we can only talk once in a while

14. Have you "cultivated a heroic self-image" that you felt deserved continuous praise or recognition from partners? If so, write about this.
15. Did you present an image of a person of stature to the world but still felt unlovable, incapable, or unworthy?
16. Did you know why you were loved in any of your relationships or did you always believe you were conning partners? Write about this.
17. Write about how having the courage to risk being known can lead to a feeling of love-worthiness (S.L.A.A. Basic Text, page 156)
18. Write a fear inventory about entering into a new sexual relationship. (See The Reconciliation Project, page 12, question number 6 for fear inventory format.)
19. Write about a relationship that was a "sexual oasis in the midst of an emotional desert (S.L.A.A. Basic Text, page 157)" in the past. How do you avoid this in sobriety?
20. What is sexual contact under false pretenses?
21. What's the difference between lovemaking and love-showing? (S.L.A.A. Basic Text, page 158)

Conclusion

Read the S.L.A.A. Basic Text, page 158 (after asterisk to page 159).

1. Does this chapter convey a sense of hope to you? Write about any glimmer of hope that arose in you.
2. Do you believe that a life of fulfillment, richness and mystery awaits in sobriety?
3. Write about the last sentence of the chapter: "We are all joint travelers on destiny's path, and we all have much to learn from each other." (page 159)
   a. What's the significance of calling ourselves joint travelers?
   b. Destiny's path implies that some kind of higher Power has a plan for your life — write about what you think the plan is for you since joining S.L.A.A.
   c. What can we learn from each other in S.L.A.A.? Write about learning truths about yourself from hearing another member share similar feelings in a meeting.

Part II – Pamphlets & other resources

Romantic Obsession*

Many of us come to Sex and Love Addicts Anonymous because of some form of obsession. Romantic obsession is broadly defined as an unhealthy fixation on another person with whom we may or may not have a relationship or even have met. A romantic obsession can be triggered by a sexual obsession, the beginning or ending of a relationship, or for reasons beyond our present understanding. The object of our romantic obsession, for example, can be someone we've heard speak at a meeting, a public figure, or an anonymous person in a magazine ad. In many cases, we may not be clear what triggers us.

The addictive nature of obsession can distort our thinking and behavior and can lead us in a direction that violates our dignity and personal integrity.

We who are plagued with romantic obsession have found hope and recovery in S.L.A.A. The program shifts the focus from the idealized romantic relationship that our disease craves to a working relationship with a Power greater than ourselves. By working the Twelve Steps of S.L.A.A., we counter the destructive behaviors and self-hatred that accompany obsession and begin to experience a gradual yet persistent return to sanity.

Once we become willing to surrender to our powerlessness and take healthy action, we can be guided safely back to sanity and released from the bondage of romantic obsession. The following are some ways that obsession can affect us.

Engaging in Romantic Obsession
Distorts our Perceptions

In the height of our obsession, we may
  • see the object of our obsession as someone other than who s/he really is.

- idealize, glorify, and give power to the other person.
- demonize or resent the object of our obsession.
- project qualities onto the person that s/he doesn't have.
- delude ourselves in our thinking and deny our disease.
- convince ourselves that we'll die without the other person.

Romantic Obsession Obscures Reality

While obsessed we may tell ourselves

- the object of our obsession can make us feel secure and content.
- our peace of mind depends on them acknowledging us or giving us what we want.
- we "love" the other person even though we may not respect his or her limits, shortcomings or boundaries.
- the other person represents a lifestyle we want but are being denied.
- our current friendships are flat and meaning- less.
- the other person is judging us and has found us a failure, inadequate or pathetic.
- we should be loyal to the other person even if s/he ignores, hurts or violates us.
- other people can't understand our pain.

Romantic Obsession Promotes Self- Destructive Behaviors

While obsessed we may find ourselves

- trying to rescue, fix or control someone with the expectation that we will get commitment, loyalty or obedience in return.
- lying about our motives, trying to manipulate or coerce others, initiating or engaging in power games or violating people's privacy and personal boundaries.
- using sex to get attention, to manipulate, to exploit, to reward or control.
- having sex even if we don't want it.

20

• engaging in sexually compulsive behavior, pornography, multiple sexual relationships, dangerous behavior, or sexual anorexia in an effort to escape emotional pain.

Romantic Obsession Stops Us from
Fully Engaging in Life

While obsessed we often
- prevent ourselves from setting goals or moving towards them.
- cut ourselves off from other people.
- restrict our behavior, narrowing it to a few monotonous routines.
- lose our interests and our interest in life itself.
- find ourselves feeling impotent, flat and lifeless.
- subvert, derail, undermine and block ourselves from emotional growth.

Romantic Obsession is
Self-Negating

At the height of our obsessing we may
- tell ourselves our life has no purpose, value or future.
- deny our real accomplishments and abilities.
- tell ourselves we're undesirable, unlovable, sexless and unworthy.
- isolate ourselves from others and experience loneliness and pain.
- compare ourselves with those who appear to "have it all".
- tell ourselves we're helpless and defeated.
- destroy any sense of purpose or mission we may have had.
- distort our personalities, making ourselves victims, liars, cheats or even violent.

Romantic Obsession is Fear-Based

We open ourselves to fears of
- abandonment and rejection.

21

- loneliness.
- humiliation.
- undesirability and uselessness.
- destruction.
- being responsible for ourselves.
- committing to others.
- committing to our recovery.

Obsession invariably leads to
- denial.
- delusional thinking.
- personal acts of dishonesty (e.g., manipulation, intrusion on others' privacy, etc.)

Here are some strategies that we have used to overcome obsession.

We
- work the 12 Steps.
- practice humility and admit we're powerless over the object of our obsession and the feelings of obsession themselves.
- pray and meditate knowing that God wants us to live free of shame, isolation, self-hatred and fear.
- ask our Higher Power to relieve our obsession.
- make an inventory of our fears.
- make a list of our accomplishments, strengths and talents.
- detach and avoid the object of our obsession "one day/one hour at a time".
- request a temporary no contact agreement.
- practice healthy vulnerability by sharing at meetings, getting and regularly calling a sponsor, and providing outreach "to the addict who is still suffering".
- engage in self-care by pursuing interests we enjoy.
- welcome healthy interests and healthy people into our lives.
- set top-lines for ourselves by focusing on what we want to add to our work, home life, and relaxation.
- find and re-confirm our purpose or mission in life.

• seek opportunities to be of service.

In our experience, there is a common pattern in sex and love addiction of delusional thinking and self destructive behavior that is fueled by obsession.

We Have Found There is a Common Solution.

We

• stop acting out on a daily basis.
• abstain from self-punishment and self-rejection.
• go to meetings.
• surrender to the pain and discomfort of withdrawal.
• work the 12 Steps of S.L.A.A.!

1. List obsessions you've had with:
   a. people you haven't met
   b. people you have met
   c. people you were in a relationship with
   d. people you weren't in a relationship with.
2. Take each section of this pamphlet and write about ways romantic obsession:
   a. *Distorted your perception:* idealizing, demonizing, projecting qualities onto someone, denying we have a disease, thinking we'll die without our obsession.
   b. *Obscured reality:* thinking we need our obsession to feel safe, thinking we are in love even if we don't like the person, life is dull without them, feeling insecure
   c. *Made you engage in self-destructive behaviors:* rescuing, lying, using sex.
   d. *Stopped you from fully engaging in life:* not setting goals, cutting off from other people, restricting behavior
   e. *Caused you to be self-negating:* life has no purpose, denying accomplishments, putting ourselves down and isolating
   f. *Caused fear:* write about each of the fears listed in the "Romantic Obsession is Fear-Based" section of the pamphlet
3. Read the strategies to overcome obsession. How many of these do you use? Write about them and how they are working for you.

Before Dating

1. Some sponsors suggest finishing a Fifth step before dating. Some say finish all steps. What seems like a reasonable time frame after withdrawal to begin dating? Write about this.

2. How do you feel about online dating versus meeting people through friends or face to face interactions only? List your fears. Write a fear inventory about anything important.

Online dating fears	Meeting people face to face only

3. Do you want to create a dating plan? Write a pros and cons list. Identify the addict voice in your list (example: pro: that I will get a perfect relationship if I do a dating plan. Identifying the addict voice and replacing it with the sober voice: a dating plan won't necessarily give me a relationship, it's just in place to help me stay sober in the dating process. No relationship is perfect.)

(Un)Sober Dating Characteristics

The following chart and Tools for Sober Dating (pages 29-34) were submitted by an S.L.A.A. member. They are included here for discussion. They reflect some members' views on sober dating. Take what you like and leave the rest.

Unsober Dating Characteristics	Sober Dating Characteristics
We act in isolation, making dating decisions without the input or support of our S.L.A.A. community. We date without a dating plan created with sober and respected S.L.A.A. members.	We make dating decisions using the suggestions of sober or trusted program members, our sponsors, and our Higher Power.
We operate from a place of scarcity thinking, assuming that good partners are few and far between.	We operate from a place of faith; we believe a loving Higher Power has given us many potential partners.
We arrange dates willfully, in a way that decreases self-care. We book dates on top of regular 12 step meeting times or other self-care times.	We schedule dates using our Higher Power's guidance. We ensure our needs are met before involving ourselves with others.
Out of fear, we people-please, tell lies or exaggerate on dates or leading up to them. We may become too sexual too fast out of fear of losing the person or out of overwhelming sexual desire.	We are courageous and direct with our dating partners, while also being considerate and respectful.
We behave on the date in a way that is not consistent with our true or higher self.	We feel good about ourselves after the date. We like who we are after the date. We do not feel high, abandoned, or frustrated.

26

Unsober Dating Characteristics	Sober Dating Characteristics
We do not practice moderation. We over-share, over-drink, over-spend time getting ready, and over-spend time and money on the date. We get willful and do not consult with Higher Power or program members about the frequency of dates. Conversely, we can under-prepare, under-give, and withhold.	We act in a right-sized way while dating. We increase physical and emotional intimacy gradually. We are mindful of our resources and do not hurt ourselves.
We date people who are unpredictable in their availability, do not treat us well and who, more often than not, do not show respect for our feelings, time, and preferences.	We date people who are available emotionally. We stay aware of yellow, orange and red flags (see List of Yellow, Orange, and Red Flags on page 33 for explanation) and share them with our sponsors or trusted members.
Alternatively, we can be demanding, disrespecting others' feelings and preferences, and get pleasure by lording over dates who we perceive as inferior.	We are respectful of all dates, even if it appears the connection is not going to work for us. We are direct but kind when moving on.
We willfully date one person at a time, fixating on a single connection or we live in isolation and cut ourselves off from any dating options.	We keep our eyes and options open when in the early stages of dating. As the field gets narrowed down, we, in a right-sized way, show up for increasing connection with the remaining dating partner.
We decrease basic spiritual care: meditation, meeting attendance, and prayer.	We maintain a healthy program life and, on top of that, a balanced life in general. We have experienced that the foundation for a life well-lived is rooted in the 12 steps and regular use of the S.L.A.A. tools.

Unsober Dating Characteristics	Sober Dating Characteristics
We fail to get important information before moving ahead. We don't get clarity on big issues such as having children, financial health, staying in the area, and commitment.	We trust in God and in the program. We have seen that only good things come when we turn our lives and our will over to the care of God.
On the date, out of fear, we numb out or amp up with alcohol, sugar, overeating or caffeine.	We turn to God as our source and refrain from acting out on compulsive behaviors, both avoidant and addictive.

1. How many of the (un)sober dating characteristics have you engaged in? Write about this.

2. How many of the sober dating characteristics have you engaged in? Write about this.

Tools for Sober Dating

Dating Plan

A dating plan is a document usually created with the help of a sponsor or a program elder. It can contain a schedule of "what can happen when." For example, "nothing more than a cheek kiss on first date" or "French kissing is allowed on date four." Some people have their plan broken into two phases, "Phase One" and "Phase Two" of dating - with phase one being in public and with minimal physical contact and phase two being after a certain number of dates or weeks and moving into the private realm of one another's homes, with increased physical and emotional intimacy.

Some members have a dating plan that includes seeing a candidate for one date a week and seeing multiple people simultaneously. Time limits for dates can also be set. For example, a first date of one hour.

The dating plan can also include the toplines we want to maintain while dating, a partner ideal checklist, and a reminder of our S.L.A.A. bottom lines. These can serve as sobering reminders about what really matters, helping to break any fantasy or addiction we have around a compelling candidate. In our experience, sobriety always comes before the pursuit of an attractive candidate.

Some members have included a break-up or termination plan in their dating plan — setting forth how they conduct themselves during a break-up or terminating a dating connection. The plan can include a list of valid reasons to break up with a dating candidate. Some of us suffer from anorexia and will leave a promising candidate for reasons that may not be healthy for us or even true (addiction may have twisted our thinking). Others stay in destructive dating scenarios due to active sex or love addiction (or both). The break-up plan is created before a candidate arrives on the scene, so that we can be assured we are making program-guided decisions.

Dating Log

The dating log can include a wide variety of facts about our dates,

Example:

- topics discussed on the date
- yellow/orange/red flags detected
- clothes the candidate or we ourselves wore
- who arrived on time or late?
- the location of the date and who selected it
- how date expenses were handled
- how we felt before, during and after going into the date
- where or how we met the candidate
- what words were exchanged at the end of the date
- how long the date lasted
- whether we would like to see the person again
- note how much we adhered to our plan
- what tools we used before, during and after the date

Sticking to the facts helps us stay out of fantasy and helps us make better decisions around possible future dates. We can also review our log from time to time and look for any patterns or recurring issues that may need to be addressed. One member saw that alcohol was a recurring problem — drinking two drinks on a date led her to more easily go off of her dating plan. Also, she saw that intensity early on was a red flag — often indicating a situation wherein "fast doesn't last." We can also use the log to monitor our progress, seeing how we are learning and growing in sober dating.

Book-ending

A bookend is a call to a sponsor, "dating buddy" or program fellow before and after the date. It may include our current feelings, some facts about the dating candidate, and our commitments to our sober dating plan. Often, we commit to a certain time duration for the date, a commitment not to drink or a maximum number of drinks, off-limits topics (e.g. recovery, childhood trauma, past relationships on early-on dates), and off-limits physicality (e.g., "no kissing" or "all clothes stay on.") and off-limits rooms ("no going into the bedroom"). It is important to hold ourselves accountable by sharing our success in achieving and maintaining our commitments or our incapacity to do so.

Dating Buddy

A dating buddy is an S.L.A.A. program fellow to call once a day, or as needed, to help you stay on your dating plan. The dating buddy can be someone with more or less time in the program than you, but it's best to have someone close to your experience level so that it feels balanced and supportive. The call to the dating buddy can include that day's commitments towards staying active in sober dating, a report on recent dates, bookends for any dates that day, a reality check on the tools one is using to sober date, and any threats to sobriety. Supportive feedback, usually in the form of experience, strength and hope and helpful suggestions can help members stay on the sober dating path. Our dating buddy's shares can trigger a wide variety of feelings: fear, judgment, shame, jealousy, arousal — all sorts of feelings may come up. This is natural and does not mean that the partnership needs to be terminated. If the sharing is not helpful to one's recovery, then it might be wise to move on to another buddy. More often though, the dating buddy arrangement provides a time of connection, laughter, support, and hope. Joy comes in as shame is reduced.

Literature, Reading, and Research — Conference-approved and Commercial Literature

Reading up on sex and love addiction, as well as dating in general, helps familiarize us with our disease and the wider dating landscape, an arena often intimidating to those of us sober dating for the first time. Learning dating etiquette and norms can be empowering and get us out of fear and helplessness. Gathering information builds confidence and makes us more likely to enjoy the date. Of course, the ultimate authority is a loving God, and even if a popular website says something is the norm, it may not serve us and our sobriety. Staying connected to S.L.A.A. literature reminds us that we have a serious disease, that we are powerless over it and that we are not alone. It helps take the focus off the dating candidate and put it back on ourselves and our Higher Power. Research, especially around online dating, helps us understand the dating marketplace and can empower us. We may learn of a new website for people over fifty or learn that certain profile pictures are considered a turn-off to many. We can get out of frustrating, self-sabotaging behavior. Some of us have shown our online dating profiles to friends in and out of the program to get feedback. We don't have to do this alone and learning about the process can be fun. Conversely, some have found that research and reading can lead to obsession and control. As with anything, we have found that sharing what's going on for us with program fellows helps guide us towards what tools and what amounts serve us. The most healing research is often calling various people who are dating in S.L.A.A.

Reality Lists
Similar to the dating log entries, this is a listing of the facts.

Reality lists can be used in instances of obsession when we are unclear whether to stay with or leave a certain candidate. It can be especially helpful to turn over the reality list to a trusted member for feedback. The reality list can include the words the dating candidate said to us, the actions they have taken in the dating context, the words we are hearing from third parties about them, data they report on any online dating profile or online context, gifts they have presented us with — any number of facts and objective information we can find. It's helpful to provide a balanced account — noting both positive and negative attributes. Many of us sway between being too condemning and too lenient. Sharing the list with others we trust can help shed some light on whether we are being mistreated or not.

List of Yellow, Orange, and Red Flags

Some members compiled a list of colored flags to look for. Yellow means proceed with caution. Orange means slow down to a complete stop and talk to lots of program people before proceeding. And red means stop the dating arrangement altogether. Everyone has their own HP and sense of what is yellow, orange or red. We have found it helpful to know what the flag categories are before going out on the dating scene. We also see that we learn as we go and can adjust or expand the lists accordingly.

Letters to God

This is something some members have done when they don't want to give up a dating candidate they are addicted to. They write about what they insist God gives them if the dating candidate is taken away. Lists include certain types of cars, a certain body weight, certain items of beautiful clothes, career advancements, beach getaways. Some have found it useful to write a response as if God was answering us. A response from

God could be, "Yes! I would love to give you these things. Let's work together!" This writing helps members see that God does not get angry if we are acting like kicking and screaming children who are upset at not getting their drug of choice. God is just happy to hear from us and happy to see us making progress towards sobriety. Some members write about their resentments against God. Writing a letter to God can help us recognize character defects, refine our concept of a Higher Power, and believe that our Higher Power loves and supports us. For those of us who don't believe in God, this exercise, or others like it can help us with Step 2 when we "act as if" God exists.

1. Take each of the 8 tools listed here (Dating plan, dating log, book-ending, dating buddy, literature, reality lists, lists of flags, and letters to God):
   a. Would you or do you use this tool?
   b. Do you think anything would be triggering if you used this tool?
   c. Write about your feelings when you read this tool.

Sample Dating Plans

These sample dating plans are compilations from different S.L.A.A. members' dating plans.

Dating plan "A"

Know each other as friends for at least 2 months.

Full disclosure of S.L.A.A. program and dating plan before dating.

Bookend dates with sponsor (Call before and after)

Date 1: coffee during the day 1 or 2 hours at the most. No physical contact. Treat it like a business meeting, light and polite, no graphic language, trauma bonding or "hooks" (rainchecks or promises to catch their attention or keep them around).

One week in between each date. We could talk on the phone but for an hour at the most once a day or so. No marathon phone sessions and no calls after 10 p.m.

Date 2: At night, dinner, or a movie. We could hold hands.

Date 3: One kiss goodnight.

Date 4: Nothing below the waist.

Date 5: We could have sex if we had a commitment, an AIDS test (We had to go together to the test.) (We had already had the STD talk.) and an acceptable method of birth control (acceptable to sponsor).

Dating plan "B"

Before you start the dating plan, go on three self-loving dates: 1. Date with God. 2. Date with yourself. 3. Date with friends. Pay attention to any feelings that come up.

Make a list of 10 non-negotiables, 5 must haves and 5 can't stands

When you start dating:

5 phone dates before meeting.

First 5 dates are double/group dates

No kissing on the first 5 dates (sponsor says kissing usually makes us high and not present to listen and really get to know someone. We are seeking an intellectual and emotional connection, not a chemical reaction. So, saying, "No kissing before the 6th date helps you get to know someone slowly. Check your motives. Are you afraid of a bad reaction if you don't kiss on the first date?)

1 year of friendship while dating

No sex before marriage

No talk of marriage in the first year.

Each dating plan should be fitted to the individual (just as bottom lines are different for different people).

1. Write about these dating plans:
    a. Is dating plan A too fast for you?
    b. Does dating plan B seem too strict?

c. Do you fear the disease of sex and love addiction will get to you if you are less strict with your dating plan?
2. What seems like a good time frame for physical intimacy?
3. How do you feel about marriage? Staying single? Having children?
4. Discuss these plans with your sponsor:
    a. Do you need more time between dates?
    b. How long before physical contact?
5. Define your idea of getting sexual.
6. How long before you get sexual with the person? What needs to be in place before you get sexual with them?
7. Would you date someone in your recovery rooms, workplace or living space (apartment complex or neighborhood)? Why or why not? Ask a sober S.L.A.A. member about their experience with this.
8. Is there anyone who is or should be romantically off limits (the ex-partners of your friends, your co-workers, your boss)? Make a list and discuss it with your sponsor.
9. Should you take some time off dating after ending a relationship? If so, how much? If not, why not?
10. Is everyone you've had a sexual or romantic relationship with on your no contact list? Write about this: list reasons why they should be on a no contact list and reasons they shouldn't be on the list and why you don't think it's a good idea to put them on the list at this time.
11. Is the idea of putting all exes on a no contact list anorexic or healthy? Write about and discuss with your sponsor any feelings that come up.

12. Define stalking. Are there dating behaviors that you engage in that could trigger stalking for you or are borderline stalking?
13. Do you feel too damaged to date?
14. Make a list of deal breakers (I cannot continue to date this person if... e.g. he's a smoker).

Suggestion: Write out your own dating plan before you begin to date.

Dating

1. Are you assigning magical qualities to your date?
2. Are you having feelings of inferiority?
3. Are you beating yourself up for something you said or did during the date or a phone conversation?
4. Is status more important than substance?
5. Are you more interested in power struggles or achieving your potential?
6. Define safe sex.
7. Discuss your idea of viewing people as objects. What can you do in your dating life to prevent this behavior?
8. Discuss perfectionism as it relates to dating.
9. List your boundaries. (e.g. No inviting strangers to my apartment. No accepting abusive behavior. No spending more money than is reasonable. No allowing manipulation.)
10. List your character defects specific to dating.
11. Are there any life experiences or things about your past you should disclose to potential partners?
12. Fill out the following chart:

	Yes	No	Why or why not?
1. I want to pay for the first ____number of dates			
2. I expect to be paid for on dates if he/she has asked me on the date.			

3. I would go to a date location whether I could afford it or not			
4. I will text with potential dates			
5. I will date more than one person at a time			
6. I will dress up / dress down for dates (circle one)			

After Date Checklist

To get out of obsession, I will:

_____ take a walk

_____ run errands

_____ do some Step work

_____ call a fellow

_____ read the Romantic Obsession pamphlet

_____ write a reality list

_____ write the name of this person and put it in my God box

_____ other: _____

Perfectionism that cropped up:

_____

Red flags (Things I probably shouldn't put up with):

_____

Yellow flags (Things I might want to be wary of):

_____

Green flags (Things that are a good sign that I should keep dating this person)

_____

Fantasies I engaged in (thoughts)

_____

Realities I saw:

_____

Character assets: (Mine and my date's)

_____

Character defects

_____

Mistakes

_____

Did anything go against my dating plan/boundaries?

_____

Dating triggers

_____

Signs person I am dating is available/unavailable

_____

Partnership

1. Are you trying to prevent your partner from trying new healthy life experiences?
2. Are you trying to control or rescue your partner?
3. Is the relationship depleting your energy or is it helping you?
4. Do you double date or go to social functions?
5. Will you be OK if the relationship doesn't work out? What actions will you take to maintain your sobriety?
6. During arguments, how would you feel about asking yourself, "Would I rather be right or happy?" Write about this.

Relationship Worksheet

Purpose of this worksheet:
To help S.L.A.A. members work with their sponsor to discuss their relationship openly and honestly, to gain some clarity about themselves and their partner, and to discover if infatuation has turned into obsession. This worksheet attempts to discover whether or not a healthy relationship has turned into an addictive/harmful relationship.

1. Have you caught him/her in a lie? Yes ___ No ___ If yes: how many times? _____ Describe each situation and its importance.
2. Do you make excuses for him/her? Describe.
3. Does he/she take a long time to call you back or break dates often without explanation?
4. Do you find it impossible to ignore phone calls or demands from this person even if it's inconvenient or harmful to you?
5. What do you think will happen if you ignore demands?
6. Do you feel unsafe because of anything he or she has done? Explain.
7. Are you able to communicate feelings to this person without fear of repercussions?
8. If not, what kind of repercussions have you suffered?
9. Does your partner give as well as receive, or are you always the giver even if it's harmful to you?
10. If so, do you fear the loss of the relationship if you quit giving so much?
11. Is there room for other activities or people in your life or does this person take up all of your time?
12. What would happen if you spent less time with them?
13. Is your partner jealous? If so, describe.

14. Do you play games to keep them more interested? If so, describe.
15. Are you playing a role around them? If so, what would happen if you were honest.
16. Have you broken up with or had no contact rules before? If so, how many times?
17. During the time you are waiting for contact, what goes through your mind? (List positive and negative fantasies.)
18. Who have you used or manipulated in his or her life to get closer to them? Describe:
    a. Physically: (getting close to parents and friends).
    b. Secretly: (stalking on social media/being an overly curious investigator?)
19. Has he or she ever physically harmed you?
20. Does anything he or she does or says make you question your own sanity? Write about this.

Suggestion: Discuss with your sponsor if your answers to these questions add up to an addictive, unhealthy situation. If so, discuss a way to proceed with a no contact rule.

Part III - ARTICLES

Reading and Questions for "Sober Dating: Articles from *the Journal* with a focus on sober dating." **(original print version available at https://store.slaafws.org/prod/JOUR003-07.html)**

MY EXPERIENCE OF DATING

I remember my sponsor telling me that "An S.L.A.A. member learning to date is like learning to walk a tiger." That has been my experience in my 4 ½ years of recovery and close to three years of what started out as sober dating and has turned into a relationship that has lasted for two years so far.

The cornerstones for refining my dating experience were, first and foremost, a detailed dating plan that covered all aspects of the dating experience.

When designing my dating plan, my sponsor and I basically took everything that I was doing that was "unhealthy," turned it upside down and redefined it into a sane and sound ideal for my dating experiences.

For instance: Prior to coming to S.L.A.A., I wouldn't think twice about entering a man's home and picking him up for our first date. What I realized was that this behavior set me up to act out on the very first date even before leaving the house for dinner!

So, by looking at this behavior, one of my dating plan goals was "no going into another man's house when dating for at least the first four dates."

It may sound rigid, but it has worked and kept me protected from unexpected triggers and temptation.

Another habit I discovered was that I would reveal very private information to men I was attracted to very early on in the experience. I would not think twice about revealing my alcoholism, my drug addiction, my bi-polar diagnosis, and on and on. I thought I was being transparent and honest, but my sponsor pointed out that I was creating a false sense of intimacy by disclosing too much information to someone I barely knew. And with that false sense of intimacy comes the possibility of my believing the relationship is more serious than it really is.

So we turned this behavior upside down and created a dating plan goal that was "no revealing intimate information such as my 12-Step programs" for at least the first four dates and that such information was to be given in piecemeal – not all at once.

Another part of my sober dating included changing my definition of what a "date" is. I had always had self-serving ideals about a date being about my finding the guy that fits my needs or makes me feel complete (the "Spark.")

My sponsor told me that initial dating is about my being of service to someone else and showing up and listening to them to gather information.

By doing this, I would find out enough to know if I felt like having a second date. I also learned that the idea that there should be some "spark" on the first date was old thinking.

In fact, I was told literally by my sponsor and therapist "If you feel sparks on the first date, run the other way!" In fact, I can't remember feeling a moment of a "spark" in my current relationship.

What developed was an intimacy that grew from many weeks' worth of one date at a time. One day, I realized that a fondness had developed for this person.

Of course, I have many other goals that I've included in my sober dating/relationship life. They include: 1) no sex until a commitment has been discussed and established (this had an underlying ideal as well that I was not to discuss commitment until at least 6 to 8 dates. Otherwise, I would commit myself to someone and be off and running within a month); 2) No sex until a frank discussion of STD status and both of us getting tested and sharing our results. 3) Allowing at least 3 days between the last date and calling for the next date (which meant not planning date number two while on date number one.)

At the end, my dating experiences and my relationships had to allow room to be "human," allowing room for mistakes, uncomfortable conversations, and having patience with myself and others. Again, it was like walking a tiger.

Also, I had to have regular contact with my sponsor, and I had to work all the Steps prior to dating. Regular meeting attendance was required. And I needed to date myself (going to places by myself and learning to enjoy my own company). Most importantly, a relationship with my Higher Power played a key role in the dating process.

It's been a bumpy and uncomfortable process at times; but I truly feel it would have been next to impossible to do it in a somewhat healthy manner had I not had the S.L.A.A. program and all its resources to guide me every step of the way.

— From *the Journal* Issue #141

Questions:

1. Do you agree with the statement that learning to date is like learning to walk a tiger? Write about this.
2. List your unhealthy dating habits in one column on a sheet of paper. Create a second column with the opposite of that habit. How can you heal that behavior?
3. Do you reveal too much to dates or people you are interested in dating? How can you keep it light and polite?
4. Define what a "date" is to you (i.e. fact-finding mission, time to have fun, etc.) List motives involved in dating for you.

5. Why do you think the writer's sponsor told them that if they felt sparks on the first date to run the other way? Is this something you feel now or have felt that you should do? Write about this.

6. Does the method of dating that the author describes in this article sound difficult to you? Describe how you would feel dating this way.

7. What are your goals for your dating or relationship life?

8. What happens if these goals aren't met?

9. Do you allow room for mistakes in dating for yourself? For your date? Describe any experiences with this.

10. Do you think regular contact with your sponsor is important while dating? Explain.

RECOVERY IN THE ELDER YEARS

I hit my bottom in March of 2011, having just celebrated my 72nd birthday. My marriage of fourteen years had fallen apart and attempts at reconciliation failed. My therapist said she thought I was a sex addict and recommended the local group of S.L.A.A. Shortly after attending a meeting, I experienced an overwhelming moment of truth that my sex addiction and emotional dependency had completely controlled my life, and it terrified me. So, there I was, already in my seventies, never having had an honest and healthy relationship with sex as a by-product of commitment, collaboration and sharing in a partnership.

The following meeting a member offered to be my sponsor. He turned out to be my Higher Power's third great gift to me (after my counselor and that gracious moment of terror). I began to work the Steps with a man who loved me unconditionally, shared his experience strength and hope, and was absolutely hard-nosed about the work.

I had a lot of pain to let go of, years of acting out with masturbation to fantasies and running away from any healthy relationship into sexual anorexia, constructing a false self that hid my secret life with all its shame, guilt and lack of control.

I became a successful college professor and massaged my ego by enlarging my resume but depended upon the approval of others to assuage that nagging feeling that I was really a failure.

The Twelve Steps came to be my way out. My sponsor patiently and firmly led me through the process of healing. His unconditional love mirrored to me the love of the God of my understanding, and I came to realize that my Higher Power had all along been my gracious Guide and Protector.

Steps Four and Five were difficult, painful, and liberating;

51

Steps Eight and Nine brought me to admit, apologize, and let go. Along the way I learned to forgive myself — and, to experience a spiritual awakening that I seek daily to nurture.

So, here I am today, just now having celebrated my 77th birthday, and having discovered true intimacy in relationships with friends, old and new, who have brought so much joy into my life. Some are also in recovery, others are not, but all have responded with pleasure to the transformation that has brought me, day by day, a new way of living.

They are teaching me what true intimacy is, and preparing me for the day when, if it be my Higher Power's will for me, a loving, romantic relationship may enrich my life.

I am preparing to put myself forward on an on-line dating service and to explore, step by step, the possibilities of a true, committed relationship. Thanks to S.L.A.A. and its program of recovery, I am now enjoying a life in which the "Promises" have come true.

My first therapist told me years ago that "it's never too late." How right she was! I hope that others will be encouraged to enrich their elderhood by making their Twelfth Step a gift of their years of wisdom and experience, a life of service to others as spiritual elders, with all the joys that come with such a life.

— From *the Journal* Issue #160

Questions:

1. How do you feel about getting older? Do sex and love addicts face special challenges? If so, write about this.
2. How do you feel or think you will feel about dating after a certain age (40, 50, 60, or in the elder years - over 65)? Write about the idea that "it's never too late."
3. Look over your answers to question 9 in the previous article (about mistakes). Have you learned to forgive yourself for

everything in your life? What are you holding on to? Write about this.

4. What does collaboration and sharing in a partnership mean to you? Have you ever had this? How do you or did you attain this?

5. List any gifts that Higher Power has given you.

6. List pain that you have let go of. Is there anything more that you need to let go of?

7. Did you achieve outward success (power, prestige, fame) but still felt like a failure? Write about this.

DATING AFTER RECOVERY

I'm not exactly a novice at dating. Since my teenage years, dating had been an intriguing ritual, an addictive dance, which I had carefully crafted. It didn't matter whether the men were married or not. My marital state didn't matter either.

Fortunately, after six years in S.L.A.A. recovery, I've made changes. I no longer date married men, an improvement in my pattern, but other changes were subtler.

I spent quite some time working on loving and accepting myself. Wait, I'm jumping ahead. It was first necessary for me to discover my authentic self before I could proceed to love and accept that relative stranger buried deeply within me. For years, I'd sacrificed my interests, my joys, and my essence to become the person that my significant other wanted me to be.

I became the mirror reflection of him. He liked football, so I popped popcorn and iced down the drinks. I quickly learned the difference between a field goal and an extra point kick. I did my homework and as I became who I thought he wanted, it got easier and easier to let go of my love of dancing, theatre, art museums.... I watched and felt myself dissolving.

The author of our Basic Text reinforces this concept when he says, "In truth, the option to 'tailor ourselves' to meet the expectation of another was untenable. Too much of our lives during the addiction had been built on just such a strategy, in the absence of possessing any real sense of who we were as people. We could not now, nor could we ever, sustain a relationship in which we had to destroy an essential part of ourselves in order to render ourselves more desirable to the eyes of another. No thanks" sex and Love Addicts Anonymous, p. 154.

After my divorce, it took some time, but I was proud to find the pearl buried within that hard, crusty shell. I made a long list

55

of my passions and nudged myself to make those things my priorities. I even reached the point where attending a movie alone was no longer sheer torture but an indulgent treat. I learned to relax in warm, luxurious bubble baths by candlelight at the end of a particularly hard day, and eventually I relished this time alone. I breathed in the aroma of the candles, listened to classical music on the stereo and slowly got to know the woman I am, the woman I've always been.

When I went through the non-dating phase, I felt comfortable making friends with men and not worrying about whether I had on make-up. I especially enjoyed knowing that I could stop sucking in my stomach and breathe freely. I could laugh and enjoy those friendships without the worries of "Will he find me attractive? Should I flirt a little more, a little less? Does he prefer all those younger women out there?" That was a comfortable stage and I wonder sometimes why I was so eager to move on. I sense that my addict was always lurking nearby for a chance to reclaim my life.

I was determined to learn from my previous mistakes. If a man didn't fit my compatibility requirements, I vowed not to waste either of our time. I had a few short relationships where I rationalized away the red flags. My sponsor continued to mention them from time to time, and I finally realized that it wasn't enough to choose a dating partner once. I had to keep choosing him: after I knew him for a couple of months, then later after we moved to a more serious level of dating. I had to continue to ask myself, "Knowing what I know now, would I still choose this person?" I had to learn to say goodbye when the answer was "No". And frequently it was.

Then I met the man I'm dating today. We spent ten weeks in a divorce recovery class together, where we slowly got to know each other as we faithfully followed the "no dating" policy. After the course ended, we had a few cautious dates. We agreed that what we both wanted was a healing relationship: a safe place where we could speak truthfully about our feelings, own our part in things without pointing the finger of blame and discover ways to celebrate our passions in life. Breaking lifelong patterns hasn't been easy over the months, but we both want this healing, so we are willing to venture outside our comfort zones. No, not venture, we are willing to live outside our level of comfort, knowing that is what it will take to experience all that we want from our relationship.

I made a vow early on in this relationship that my life would have three parts: the time I spent with my new partner, plenty of time with my friends, and, yes, even time when I'm willing to embrace the solitude. So far, with the help of my Higher Power, my sponsor, my meetings, and my community of recovery friends, it seems like this relationship could be a wonderful departure from the past. It's hard work, but it's worth it.

— From *the Journal* Issue #109

Questions:

1. Write about sacrifices you made to: A) your interests B) things that brought you joy C) your authentic self, in order to keep a relationship.
2. As described in the article, did you ever become a mirror image of a partner? If so, write about this.
3. Do you have a real sense of who you are as a person in recovery? Write about your good qualities.
4. Do you feel strong enough to resist the urge to destroy an essential part of yourself in order to render yourself more desirable to another person? If so, how did you get there and how do you maintain that feeling? If not, do you feel capable of dating? Write about all the feelings that come up.

5. Do you use the methods of self-care mentioned in the article? List any that aren't mentioned. Do you procrastinate or complain about needing to take these actions? Are you able to maintain regular self-care? If not, why not? Write about your feelings.

6. Are you comfortable with members of the same sex? Opposite sex? Write about this.

7. Are you confident in your ability to stay sober while dating? Write about this.

8. Define flirting. In what instances is flirting appropriate? Not appropriate?

9. Write about the idea that the writer of the article puts forth, that the addict is lurking nearby to reclaim your life.

10. Have you learned from previous dating mistakes? Write about these.

11. Do you have compatibility requirements? If so, list these and write about how important each of them is.

12. Write about rationalizing away red flags.

HEALTHY DATING

My focus currently is to figure out how to date in a healthy way. How do I know if something I'm doing while dating is sober? I created guidelines when I was dating many years ago. I'd been in Program and abstinent for years. Not having someone in my life had been a conscious choice. I felt good about myself and about being alone. I had a lot of serenity. I had decided it was time to put my S.L.A.A. recovery to the test. I would pay attention to everything my date did.

Actions speak louder than words. When my date seemed fully present and appeared to like me a lot, but his only contact was a brief email once weekly, I knew he wasn't emotionally available for a relationship. I would pay attention to everything my date said.

A first date once said, "Suppose you and I were to have a sexual relationship. And after a while, you came to think it was more than that. You would be hurt ..." I was stunned at his candor, arrogance and conceit; However, I was glad he was being honest, because I didn't waste any more time on him. I took him at face value and didn't try to convince myself he would change his mind once he got to know me.

I wouldn't go to my date's house unless I was willing to have sex with him.

I had gotten into trouble before by going to my date's house.

Once I narrowly avoided being attacked by my date, who believed my fighting style revealed a secret wish to be raped.

I would only have sex with someone who loved me. Believing myself to be modern, I tried the one-night stand route, only to discover it to be hollow and isolating. I would only have sex with someone I loved.

Equally important, was to love the person I allowed that

close to me. It was amazing to me that I could make that choice, and I was to learn how much nicer sex was when I loved the person with whom I was sleeping.

I would only have sex with someone who was emotionally available in a mutually committed relationship. Mutual love isn't enough, no matter how deep. The person had to be available for a relationship, which excluded anyone married, separated, or still involved with someone else.

At the first sign of abuse, the guy was history. Abuse included any kind of rudeness, standing me up, lateness that was disrespectful of my time, disappearing acts; verbal abuse, raising his voice at me, name-calling, blame, criticism, taking my inventory or trying to tell me what to do; tickling, touching after I said no, pushing, roughness, or any kind of physical force or violence.

The last time I dated, I stuck to these guidelines, amazed at how well they worked. I knew I was on the right track when I discovered that my self-esteem had increased exponentially.

The one person who passed all these tests became my husband; a relationship marked by serenity for nearly18 years.

— From *the Journal*, Issue # 106

Questions:

1. How do you know if something you're doing while dating is sober? Are you honest with yourself and fellows? Write about this.
2. Are you present enough on dates to really hear what the other person is saying? Do you take them at their word or try to change them? Describe your state of mind or challenges during dates.
3. Do you notice deal breakers or triggers on any of your dates? What is your reaction?

4. Does the last line of the article give you hope ("The one person who passed all these tests became my husband; a relationship marked by serenity for nearly 18 years.")? Write about this.

ISOLATED FROM GOD, MYSELF AND OTHERS

When I walked into anonymous programs fourteen years ago, I was isolated from God, myself, and others.

I was isolated from God because I spent most of my life either believing He didn't exist or thinking He must hate me if He did exist. I suffered a lot of verbal, physical and sexual abuse as a teenager from a nine-year relationship with a psychopath who ended up murdering my best friend. I thought if God did exist, he abandoned me a long time ago.

Through the tools of S.L.A.A. (steps, meetings, praying to a God I didn't understand and meditation even when restless) I started to see that God did exist and He hadn't abandoned me — I had abandoned Him in favor of my boyfriend. I made my boyfriend my Higher Power for nine years. Most of the time it was because of fear (because he stalked me and threatened my life). But a lot of it was staying in a bad situation because I was addicted to him.

S.L.A.A. helped me break my isolation from God and taught me to maintain conscience contact with Him daily. My sponsor had me write out what I thought God was. At that time, he was an evil man who sat up in the sky on his throne and played tricks on me. He was constantly ruining everything in my life and laughing at me. He was judging me, and I was always coming up short. My sponsor had me tear up the sheet of paper that contained that writing, symbolically throwing that God out. Then I had to write what I wanted God to be no matter how outrageous my demands.

I wanted my own personal Santa Claus who gave me everything that I wanted and who loved me unconditionally. My sponsor told me my Higher Power would love me unconditionally but that I would eventually get a more realistic God than Santa Claus. When I had a lightning-bolt spiritual experience two years later, I saw what she meant. I was insane, on my hands and knees crying and screaming and hyperventilating about a relationship with a married man. I called a fellow S.L.A.A. member and she said "Prayers are powerful. What do you want me to pray for?"

I said, "Pray for my obsession with (my qualifier) to be lifted." She said the prayer with me over the phone. I felt a calm and sanity come over me. That was my S.L.A.A. sobriety date. I was a completely different person from that day until now, nine years later.

Today, I am convinced that God does exist and works in my life as long as I seek Him and ask for His plan. He has given me the gift of sobriety and a life beyond my wildest dreams because I am free from the insanity of my addict mind.

I saw a movie once about a woman who ended up standing in the dark all alone because she refused to accept God because she suffered tragedy and her life didn't go the way she wanted it to. I don't ever want to go back to that place and feel that level of isolation from God again.

I was isolated from myself because I didn't even know myself. I was so busy trying to be the perfect daughter, girlfriend, and worker that I didn't know what I liked.

I fit my personality to the situation. If I was going to a party, I dressed up in tight clothing and played the party girl even if I was uncomfortable or cold or tired.

I didn't even have a hobby because I was too busy running around trying to make my boyfriend's lives easier.

I got good grades to impress my parents but hid that from my stoner friends. I was in honor society and cheerleading and gymnastics but was also a chain-smoker who could drink anyone under the table. I was in so many groups that I never knew which one I truly belonged to.

When I joined S.L.A.A. I had to start being honest about who

I was and what I thought. A lot of this was revealed in my Fourth and Fifth steps. My sponsor made me get a hobby.

I chose bead work. Today I make beautiful beaded necklaces.

She also forced me to take myself out on dates. I had to start thinking about what I liked to do. In the past I always went along with what my boyfriend wanted to do, even if I was bored to tears. I took myself out to movies and restaurants and art galleries.

This came in handy when in my fourth year of S.L.A.A. meetings, I started dating a guy from London. I went to visit him, and he was too busy with work to spend time with me. I took myself to all the plays and musicals I could find. I had a blast instead of sitting in his apartment stewing over his disinterest.

My sponsor also forced me to become self-supporting through my own contributions. I couldn't rely on my parents for money anymore which was a huge step for me. My self-esteem grew by leaps and bounds when I could honestly say I supported myself. And I didn't have to rely on anyone else to come and rescue me.

Rescuing usually brings control along with it.

Another big part of isolation from myself had to do with honesty. I wasn't honest with myself or anyone else. I ran around telling so many lies so that I wouldn't hurt people's feelings or get hurt myself that I no longer knew what the truth was anymore. Knowing that you're lying to people and doing it anyway because you're desperate is not self-esteem building. And keeping a bunch of stories straight doesn't leave time or room to work on getting to know yourself. I was spending so much time remembering stories that I couldn't look inside myself and really get to know myself.

Being honest in meetings and with my sponsor cleared out

all the junk in my head so I could focus on character defects and actually work on myself. I had so much more energy when I wasn't running myself into the ground with lies.

Breaking out of my isolation from myself helped me with my isolation from others.

Once I was able to trust myself and my sobriety it was easier to trust others. In my first few years in S.L.A.A. I felt like I was in a high school class. We all went to the same meetings and out for fellowship to great restaurants. We had game nights and birthday parties and anti-Valentine's Day parties. I went to potlucks and picnics and even dances. Before S.L.A.A. these events were only opportunities to find someone to hook up with. I didn't care about being real or being there for anyone, it was all about the chase.

When it's a competition it's every man (or woman) for himself. But in S.L.A.A. it was like I was a kid again, dancing with abandon and not caring if anyone thought I was a dork because I wasn't going to be able to hook up with anyone anyway. Those were the unspoken rules for those parties. I remember one party I wore a sign around my neck that I had seen Sandra Bullock wear in the movie "28 days." It said, "Confront me if I don't ask for help." My sponsee and I laughed all night about that. We had so much fun knowing that we didn't have to impress anyone, and we could ask anyone in the room for help if we needed it.

When it came to significant others, it took a lot of outside help to tackle that behemoth. But, like Ali McBeal said, "Maybe I'll share my life with somebody...maybe not. But the truth is, when I think back of my loneliest moments, there was usually somebody sitting there next to me." Being seen but not heard is very lonely.

None of the guys I was with before my recovery in S.L.A.A. ever heard me. I was never honest with them or myself, so they couldn't hear the real me anyway. S.L.A.A. helped me find the real me. And God and S.L.A.A. helped me find the man who became my husband and partner.

My sponsor gave me a dating plan that helped me show my partner the real me and gave us enough time to really get to know each other. I wasn't able to isolate myself because I had to be in constant contact with my Higher Power, sponsor and meetings. I had to do this because a healthy fear of my disease made me feel like everything would be too overwhelming otherwise. I felt like dating would break me without all the help I got from God and other S.L.A.A. members.

The difficulty with being honest and showing another human being who you really are is that they can see who you are and say "You know I really don't like that so I'm going to go now."

I suffered from post-traumatic stress that gave me panic attacks in my first year of sobriety. I dealt with my panic attacks with therapy, outreach calls and prayers. By the time I started dating in sobriety my panic attacks were much more manageable and with less frequency. They used to come in the form of blinding swirling lights. If I was on the freeway and a panic attack hit me I had to stop the car because I couldn't see — It's a good thing they only happened when I was sitting in bumper-to-bumper traffic.

With a lot of work on myself and doing the 12 Steps five times, the severe panic attacks stopped. Every once in a while, I would have what I began to call an episode. I wouldn't have attacks anymore, but I would get confused and not know where I was or what year it was. When I first began to date my now-husband, he didn't know how to handle these episodes.

My character defects of jealousy and drama queen and immaturity were also pretty hard to handle. After six months of dating, my then-boyfriend decided he didn't want to deal with it anymore. So, he broke up with me.

This was confusing to me because even though I did the dating plan and followed my sponsor's direction and felt I did everything right the S.L.A.A. way, he was still a human being with his own thoughts and feelings who could choose to walk away, which he did.

My anorexic addict voice said, "see you shouldn't trust people because even if you do everything right, they'll abandon you in the end anyway."

I told him that if he wanted to get back together to give me a call otherwise to please not contact me. I knew my addict would start trying to manipulate him to come back to me if I stayed in contact with him and tried to be "friends." I would have gone back to my dishonest codependent ways to try to change his mind. That was too much of a temptation for me.

He went away and I went to the desert to visit my family and grieve. I read the "Grief in Recovery Handbook." I was amazed that I didn't even feel like acting out or retaliating or replacing the loss. I relied on God, meetings, my family, and the fellowship of S.L.A.A. to get me through that tough time that used to break me (before sobriety in S.L.A.A. I always gained 40 pounds and became suicidal after a breakup and acted out with anyone who would have me).

And two months later —after he did some soul searching — he came back to me.

I needed that time away to realize that relationships are more about trusting God and myself than about trusting others. And it's about communication and living in reality. Once I stopped choosing dangerous men, my partners turned out to be trustworthy human beings.

I found a really good guy in sobriety (God chose him) who is willing to do the work with me. That was part of the reason he came back. He realized he had a partner who was also willing to

68

do the work.

He joined S.L.A.A. a year after we started dating and he's the chair of our local intergroup and sponsors more people than I do.

I always say that God found the perfect partner for me. He's not perfect, but he's perfect for me. I'm not that scared little girl anymore hiding in her apartment with the curtains drawn doing puzzles and smoking cigarettes all day. And sleeping on the floor at night with all the lights on because she's afraid someone will break in.

I actually like going to parties and meetings and meeting with sponsees. I like going to the beach and the park and hiking and being out in the world. People know the real me and some even like me.

I wouldn't trade what I've got today for anything and that's a good place to be. I am grateful to S.L.A.A. and God for my life.

— From *the Journal*, Issue #128

Questions:

1. Write about your isolation from God, self, and others in your lifetime.
2. Write about instances you felt abandoned by God. Was Higher Power there in these instances even though you didn't know it?
3. Did you stay in abusive relationships for a long time because of addiction? (A creative suggestion: write about important instances in a one-page story as if it happened to someone else.)
4. Write about your concept of Higher Power and your way of making conscious contact with a Higher Power.
5. Write about any spiritual experiences you have had in your life.

6. What do you think of fellowship (going to restaurants after a meeting, social functions with other S.L.A.A. members)? Does it help you? Do you shy away from it? Is anything harmful about it? Write about it and discuss it with your sponsor.

7. Do you have PTSD, panic attacks, anxiety, or clinical depression? Write about your challenges and how you deal with them.

8. Write about your dating character defects. How do you deal with them?

9. Have you gone through a sober break-up? If so, write about this. Did you have methods of dealing with grief? Did you have a no contact rule or remain friends? How did you maintain sobriety or return from a slip?

WITH S.L.A.A., I GIVE LOVE (AND DATING) A GOOD NAME!

Before I found S.L.A.A., I definitely gave love a bad name (as the song says). But with a lot of help from my sponsor and recovery partners, I've made great strides. Today, I have 17 months of sobriety in S.L.A.A. and am miraculously in a very healthy and happy relationship for the past three months. Yes, it's still young, but after being divorced for over 13 years, I've had tons of first dates. I've only dated a handful of men for one month, another handful for two months and only one for over a year. So, to make it past the two-month mark in recovery is huge for me.

To practice sane and sober dating has not been easy. I've been used to seeking the high I get from making men my everything. But that pattern always leads to the fall when they turn out to be human and the high plummets to an all-time low. With the help of the program I am so happy that I will never have to repeat this painful cycle again. I sure don't miss the despair and frustration it brought me.

Here are a few of the lessons I've learned and tools I've used for sane and sober dating:

- *I had to begin by clearly defining my dating intentions.* What were my intentions for dating at this time in my life? I was looking to date someone that could lead to a long-term relationship, possibly marriage. I was not looking to casually date. (Can we sex and love addicts even remotely do this and still be sober?) This intention set the tone for me on every date.

  If there was something about the person that I felt was not a good match for me as a long-term relationship, then there was no point in me going out with them a second time. Of

71

course, I had to be careful about my perfectionism, but overall honesty and facing reality helped.

- *My Higher Power, my program and my life have to continue to be my focus — not the person I'm dating.* If this is not the case, then I am not ready to begin dating. If at any point I see I'm unable to keep my focus on my life, my program and my Higher Power, I need to take a break. This is demonstrated by the number of meetings I attend, the number of phone calls I continue to make daily and by my dedication to my daily self-care and responsibilities. It is a red flag on me and my recovery if any of these activities change due to dating.

- *I had to give myself permission to make mistakes and learn as I go.* Dating is absolutely not for the faint of heart. Our Basic Text says that "getting into a new relationship is like putting Miracle Grow on our character defects" and it is very true. Dating is the equivalent of telling an alcoholic to go into their favorite bar and have a drink or two and then stop and go home sober. Helllloo! I don't know many recovering alcoholics who would like to try that one on for size!

  Therefore, we have to know and accept that we are going to make mistakes. We analyze the situation and have a plan for it, so that at best we can minimize the challenges and issues, but we can't prevent them completely. So, give yourself permission to make mistakes and learn as you go...just don't lose your sobriety over it. It is often bumbling before it is graceful.

- *I have to be capable of knowing when to and how to set firm boundaries for my safety and comfort.* My first summer in S.L.A.A. recovery, I went on a business trip to New Orleans.

72

My hotel was three blocks from Bourbon Street. I met a very nice man in the lobby of my hotel, and he invited me to dinner and to go dancing. I accepted. He was a perfect gentleman, and we had a lovely dinner then had a blast together dancing the night away.

Around 1:00 a.m. my feet were in excruciating pain. We had to stop dancing and I needed to go back to my room. I had to take my shoes off to walk back to the hotel and he told me he wanted to give me a foot massage. I was in so much pain that I agreed to let him come to my room and give me a foot massage.

I knew I would not allow things to get heated and turn into anything but that. I was confident. He came to my room, kissed me lightly a few times, gave me a great foot massage and then left. He wasn't even in my room an hour. The next time I spoke to my sponsor I proudly told her of this experience and waited for her accolades.

Instead, there was this long silence before she calmly replied, "Mary, you invited a stranger to your room. You didn't know this person in the slightest and he came to your room alone. You can't do that." I can't tell you how sobering her words were. Did she ever burst my smug little bubble. She revealed a pattern for me. I was way too trusting, way too soon. And I didn't set boundaries for my safety.

I was also known to get lost in relationships. I knew this tendency of mine long before I discovered S.L.A.A. but I had no idea how to change it. Boundaries provide us protection and care. They are a gift that I give myself to help me stay sane and sober while dating. They give me the freedom and structure my disease needs to be able to enjoy dating! Here are a few boundaries I've needed to be firm with: The time I

73

need to be in my own bed asleep and alone; when I'm available to talk by phone and when I'm not; how far I'm willing to go physically.

When I first began dating my current boyfriend, we were staying out too late, attending special events in neighboring cities. I was exhausted because I was frequently getting to bed too late. I phoned him in exasperation one morning and said, "Tonight I need to be in my bed alone by 11:30."

He was very accommodating. We changed our plans a little and when he dropped me off at my house, we sat on the sofa talking. At around 10:45, I saw him look at his watch and say, "I want to make sure you get to bed on time." And that is precisely what he did. It was such a gift of setting the boundary and asking for what I needed. It gave me the opportunity to see that he could think about my needs even if he wanted to spend more time with me.

He wasn't selfish and self-centered.

- *I had to learn to aim for spaciousness and avoid enmeshment.* Enmeshment is intense. It is the difference in painfully pouring down the packet of Crystal Light powder in your mouth vs. pouring the Crystal Light packet into a glass of water and enjoying how refreshing it is. Relationships are not supposed to be that intense.

Enmeshment is the cornerstone of the phrase, "We addicts don't have relationships, we take hostages!" This is one of the biggest gifts my final qualifier (the man who got me into the meetings) gave me. He told me, "You are intense." No one had ever told me that before. Now I've got an "intensity monitor" going on in my head at all times. I'm always looking for moments where I up the intensity instead of decreasing the intensity.

74

Enmeshment is demanding of the other person's time and attention. It is jealous of how and who they choose to spend their time with, instead of spending it with me. I am only supposed to be a companion or girlfriend, not a jailor, dictator or terrorist taking a hostage.

Spaciousness is freeing. I get to keep my life and enjoy getting to know someone else at the same time. With enmeshment and intensity, my world becomes tiny and entirely consumed by someone else. I am consumed with being with them, controlling them, knowing everything about them. I have to know where they are and what they are doing at all times. They have ownership of my life and I try to take ownership of theirs. I'm not even aware of the moment I do all this. Awareness of the intensity I create, or allow the other person to create, helps me to keep on solid footing with my sobriety and my program of recovery.

At first it was uncomfortable, and I would have to tell myself that this is what spaciousness in a relationship feels like. I don't know where he is or what he is doing right now, and he doesn't know where I am or what I'm doing right now and that is fantastic (even though it felt very strange)! This is how it is supposed to be. We are in a relationship; we don't own each other.

He is not my hostage, nor I, his. He is free to come and go as he pleases. I do not have the right to dictate who he sees, where he goes or what he does. Nor does he have the right to dictate any of these for me.

Before S.L.A.A., I thought enmeshment was the sign of a great relationship. Now I recognize it for the burden it truly is on me and the man I am dating.

- *I have to constantly be aware of and avoid the need to seek validation from a man.* I try to be constantly aware of the buzz, the high, the hit, I would get off of dating, compliments, and attention. If you are aware of it, you can see your disease in action and take the appropriate measures to stay grounded in reality and avoid getting sucked into the disease's downward spiral. We cannot look to others, especially those we are dating, to give us validation. We have to look to our Higher Power, to our recovery partners, to the program and to our own self-care and self-love to validate us.

- *I had to learn how to go slow and consciously practice healthy pacing in dating.* I've had so many people tell me to take it slow for a change and I really, really wanted to take it slow, I just had absolutely no idea how to do that. I'm a sex and love addict, for Pete's sake!

    So, before my recovery, I always ended up going too fast and burning out the relationship before it had the chance to get on solid footing. I thought having relationships at break-neck speed was the only way to go! As sex and love addicts, we have our own brand of "speed dating." There's no way for me to be sober and build a solid relationship "speed dating."

    I had to learn to set boundaries for myself in the areas of physical contact, phone contact, email contact, text contact, when to say "I love you," and when to introduce my child to the person. I decide these things. They aren't haphazard. They aren't random. They occur by my choice and when I'm ready, not when someone else is ready. Here are a few guidelines I use to practice healthy pacing while dating:

- I next to never call a man I'm interested in dating. And even when I'm in a relationship, I monitor it carefully allowing him to continue to pursue me and to be cautious of creating an enmeshed relationship. Too much contact too soon creates enmeshment, and it is very difficult to get un-enmeshed once you are. So, it is far better for me to resist my need for tons of contact and cultivate spaciousness from the beginning.
- I don't get off of calls just to take their call.
- I call them back by the end of the day or within 24 hours, not immediately unless absolutely necessary. Think pacing and spacing.
- If a man I'm dating calls me too early in the morning or too late at night, I don't take the call (even though I may want to). And I don't return the call until the next day or an appropriate time for me.
- I discourage texting by saying early on, "I'm not a big texter. I prefer to have predominantly phone communication and to use texting for brief communications."
- I reply to texts eventually, and rarely immediately.
- Instead of getting into an important conversation via texting, I will frequently text, "Call me when you can talk."
- I do not engage in long email communications even if they do.
- I do not engage in any sexual activity beyond holding hands and kissing for a minimum of 30 days. That means all zippers stay zipped, all snaps stay snapped, all hooks stay hooked, and if you haven't

gotten the point yet, all clothes stay on! Yes, that's a tough order, but it is one of my bottom lines and it can be done!

o   I do not engage in any sexual activity without a verbal conversation about the relationship in the light of day with both feet on the floor. We need to know each other well enough to feel comfortable committing to monogamy and not dating anyone else.

- *I dress conscientiously.* As I'm dressing for a date, I ask myself, "What am I communicating about who I am and the kind of woman I am? How on earth can I expect a man to take it slow when I'm baring ¾ of my breasts over dinner?" Now, I prefer to go with classy sexy vs. blatantly sexy. And just as a side bar, I always go to my S.L.A.A. meetings dressed as conservatively as I possibly can.

- *I practice impeccable self-care all the time.* In the past, when I've gotten lost in a relationship, I've given up important steps in my own self-care — particularly sleep. Or I don't take such great care of myself when I'm not in a relationship because it doesn't matter anyhow. I don't value myself so much unless I'm in a relationship. Not anymore. I take care of myself no matter what.

  My self-care is non-negotiable. I don't give up me to take care of thee/him. I have to take care of me first. Here's what I need regularly: The time necessary to work my program of recovery aggressively every single day, to make my recovery calls; to get adequate sleep, rest, nutrition, exercise/activity; and to have a peaceful environment and moderate pace of life to flourish in.

  How I feel and what I think matter the most. I cannot

change who I am to make certain he likes me. I have to be me and take care of myself and if he likes me great. If not, that's great too. I get to move on to someone who will be more appropriate for me.

- *I stay grounded in reality and avoid getting into my fantasy at all costs.* Enmeshment and fantasy are the deadly duo when it comes to dating. I make certain I see myself for who I am and that I see the person I'm dating for who they are, not what I want to make them up to be in my diseased mind or not who I wish they were. I'm dating a real person, not a fantasy person. I need to keep my feet firmly planted in reality. Working my program diligently every day helps me to do this. When I see red flags, I have to admit them to my sponsor and most of my recovery partners. This helps me stay in reality.

- *I avoid drinking alcohol on most dates.* It is impossible for me to keep my boundaries, practice healthy pacing and keep my focus on reality if I've had even one glass of alcohol. Therefore, I choose not to drink on most dates and when I do, I only have one glass of wine.
This is a gift I give myself. I also like to see the reaction my date has to my choice to abstain. Their response is a huge indicator of how important drinking is to them. If they are uncomfortable with me not drinking, that's a red flag to me.

- *I avoid slippery situations at all costs.* My sobriety comes first. If a situation doesn't feel right, then it probably isn't. I have the right to be comfortable and to feel safe. When a guy tells me he wants to cook me dinner at his place early on, I see the reality of the situation and tell him I will definitely look forward to that when I've gotten to know him a little bit better.

- *I accept that if I can't break up then I'm not ready to date.* Breaking up and moving on is just a part of healthy dating. Not everyone is perfect for us. I knew my breakup skills had to be excellent otherwise I would stay in unhealthy or inappropriate relationships too long. And just avoiding their phone calls is not acceptable for me.

- *And, finally, I practice "The Hippocratic Oath of Dating," which is, "Above all else, do no harm."* When it comes to dating, it is definitely a jungle out there. I do my very best not to be one of the many crazies who makes life miserable for others.

  I like to take the high road. After all, it is much less crowded up there. I try to keep it light and fun and take my time getting to know someone. There is no rush and, just like car collisions, the faster you go, the more damage you do. Dating is the same way. All of these points tie together to make for great damage control. I take care of myself and in that process, I'm usually taking better care of the person I'm dating as well.

When I put all these items into practice, I have serenity in dating. I have fun and I don't give love such a bad name. These tools help me to stay sober and actually enjoy dating whether I make a "love connection" or not.

—From *the Journal*, Issue #146

Questions:

1. Write about your ideas about what a love relationship should be.
2. Take each of the bullet points in the article about sane and sober dating and write about your thoughts and experience with each.

3. Does the way of dating described in the article seem like a fit for you? Write about any misgivings and anything that stands out for you.

ANSWERING STEP QUESTIONS

Step 2 Question: What makes you think your next relationship will be any better?

Though it's not certain whether or not I'll ever be in a relationship again (I'd prefer not), I guess hypothetically, it would be 'better' because it would no longer be between just me and some guy and no-one-else-in-the-whole-wide-world.

I would have a support team, consisting of my Higher Power, my sponsor, my S.L.A.A. fellows, and my therapist.

God would be invited into the relationship from its inception, and continuing to work my program would mean that I would need to be sharing about the relationship, throughout its lifespan, with my sponsor, in meetings, and during calls with recovery partners.

This would serve several purposes: first, I would be seeking God's will for me and for the relationship, instead of dictating my own will and ensuring that it came to pass.

I would be able to trust that God had put this person in my life, for some undetermined amount of time, and I'd be able to look at the connection as a gift from which I was meant to learn certain things and have certain experiences.

Secondly, sharing with program people would help keep the relationship transparent and non-secretive.

My fellows would be as benevolent mirrors, gently helping me to refocus my gaze when choosing to stay blind to any glaring character defects of mine that might be poisoning the relationship. As well, the transparency would allow others to see red flags that I might be missing, such as a significant other treating me disrespectfully or acting in an unavailable or uncaring way.

By the time I might be ready to date again, I would no longer feel it necessary to rush into a relationship with someone, and to assail him with charm and compliments. I would be able to love myself enough that I would not be desperate for another person to do it for me.

Therefore, there'd be a diminished or eliminated need to hook my significant other into an addictive dynamic by wearing my various masks, via acts of smoke and mirrors, and/or by demonstrating what I considered to be romantic or sexual prowess.

I would be able to trust myself to be my authentic self and know that someone else's evaluation of me should not determine my degree of lovability.

As well, having worked through some of the shame from my past, as well as childhood trauma and family of origin issues, I would also no longer need to push my significant other away, or open the relationship up and encourage him to get interested in other women, in order to hasten my inevitable abandonment.

By that time, I would have been able to come to some kind of terms with intimacy, with myself and with God, and I would be less distressed at the thought of experiencing it with another person.

Having some degree of self-awareness, finally, whereas before there was truly none, I would no longer be doomed to repeat the same sad story over and over for the rest of my life.

I wouldn't need to put myself through re-creations of childhood experiences of loss, sorrow, and disconnection – and if I were to catch myself doing it, I'd be able to recognize it for what it was (either on my own or with the assistance of others), to examine it closely and to do something about changing it.

I would not have to deal with relationship conflict, or any complicated emotions that may arise in me, on my own anymore, either.

I would have already had the opportunity to practice open, honest, and nurturing relationships with my recovery partners and sponsor over several years, and so would likely feel less fear at having to be vulnerable and honest with my significant other.

— From *the Journal*, Issue #154

Questions:

1. Write about your answers to the question posed in this article (Step 2 question from the "Step Questions Workbook:" "What makes you think your next relationship will be any better?")

2. How do you tell the difference between seeking God's will for the relationship and dictating your own will and ensuring that it comes to pass? How do you surrender your will?

DISCOMFORT IS PART OF SOBER DATING

Are you ready to experience excruciating discomfort? Get ready for sober dating! Sober dating is another opportunity to rewire all those dysfunctional neuropathways. But doing things differently is extremely uncomfortable and seemingly unnatural.

I don't want to get into all my past behaviors that landed me in S.L.A.A. We all have our pasts.

I will say that I have had my turn as addict, and I have had my turn as avoidant; my go-to was my addict.

So, my first time on the sober dating scene, I thought I was in a race.

I thought, "I can have at least one date a week. How do I make sure that I see the person I like every week?" And I ended up rushing into my first sober relationship.

It was far from my idea of the "perfect relationship" (P.S. everyone, perfect relationships don't exist.).

I was far from perfect and I felt sloppy. Learning how to show up when I didn't feel like it was hard.

Learning how to communicate in a healthy way was difficult and I felt vulnerable most of the time.

But I kept showing up, honestly, in my program.

I kept all my commitments. I finished my Steps. I kept working the Steps daily.

And in the end, I found my needs didn't match with my then partners.

So, we ended the relationship. It was the first time I had ever been in a relationship that wasn't ending because we had engaged in sh**y behavior. We just simply weren't compatible, and we were able to recognize that and walk away!

It was a little bit of a bummer not meeting someone who was more on my page, but I am so grateful for the experience.

The real purpose (I believe) of sober dating is to bring me closer to myself.

Through my imperfect experience and the challenges of navigating my first sober relationship, I had to learn how to really show up for myself. Every time I fell, I picked up a new tool of recovery.

Most importantly, I gained a psychic shift. I was finally figuring out how to meet my own needs before coming to my partner. And it was painful in many ways. It was my first experience of dating without enmeshing with my partner.

And I constantly wanted to run away. Instead, I kept showing up and doing my best.

My experience was filled with a lot of triggers, sitting with that feeling, journaling, meditating, talking with fellows, being honest in program, and really getting to the core of my feeling.

I would (and still do) ask myself, "What was my original wound? How did I get that wound? What did I need to do to take care of that wound? How can I take care of it now?" I started meeting my own needs in that way.

It was also my first time keeping the complete life I had when I started a relationship.

Not only did I keep my complete life, but because of showing up for myself throughout the relationship and asking myself what I needed, my life got even bigger.

I started going on self-dates more often.

I started signing up for classes I had always wanted to take. Swing dance? Yes, please!

Scuba diving? I love being in the water. Love letters? I love receiving affection on a nightly basis. Love letters are the biggest commitment I have made to myself so far.

I started writing them to myself 5 months ago and have made the commitment to write one every day for a whole year.

I have forgotten a day here and there. And I am allowed to

be imperfect. But I recognize that love is a committed choice. So, when I make a mistake, especially when I make a mistake, I keep showing up for myself.

Now I am dating again, at the start of a new dating process, and I have already picked up several more tools for meeting my own needs.

I am finding more peace and acceptance and showing up more compassionately, one day at a time. Dating is providing me with opportunities to love myself unconditionally.

I am still making mistakes. But I am showing up honestly through them. And that is all any of us can do on this sloppy, messy journey.

— From *the Journal*, Issue #166

Questions:

1. How do you deal with discomfort while dating?
2. How do you avoid enmeshing?
3. Write about your triggers while dating. Write about the questions posed by the writer: "What was my original wound? What do I need to do to take care of that wound?"
4. Write about the idea of writing love letters to yourself. If you dislike the idea, why? If you like the idea, will you make a commitment to do it?

NEW TOOLS FOR DATING

Dating has literally transformed from night-to-day since I've embraced the S.L.A.A. program. I have new tools that I would have never dreamed up on my own. I never knew there were several stages to dating. I thought there were just two stages: feeling awkward and then jumping into a long-term commitment. My fear of men and my own powerlessness kept me from enjoying the dating process.

Here are some of the options recovery is giving me: I meet a man for one to two hours max in the daytime for the first couple of dates. I drive my own car and meet him in a public place.

If I spend four to five hours with a new date, it's much more difficult for me to stay out of obsession. I limit the first meetings to daytime, because evening is a more vulnerable time for me due to social and cultural influences.

I can ask men I am interested in for coffee dates to initiate things. Once I start spending time with a few different men, I start feeling more confident. Then more men start to ask me out.

I look at dating as a way to develop a friendship, so I am not exclusive with one man until I decide I really like him and am ready to have a deeper relationship.

By dating a few men at a time, it keeps me from getting exclusive before I know a man well. I realize that for some in this program this is acting out behavior, but for someone like me who has jumped into long term relationships too soon it's a great tool.

I realized that, if I hadn't been dating more than one man, I could have easily gotten exclusive with any one of them. I obsess less if I am developing friendships with more than one man. It's easy for me to go into a sense of scarcity, thinking this one man is my only option. This helps me to be more selective.

I do my best to stay in the present, reminding myself constantly that I do not really know this person yet. If I start fantasizing about a future with him, I lose my ability to stay present and see if I really like him. Instead of focusing on, *does he like me?* I focus on, *Do I like him?* This way I am looking out for my own well-being.

I talk to my sponsor before and after every male contact. Sometimes I talk to her answering machine (I get her permission first). I don't tell my whole life story to a man until I get to know him a little better. Once I decide I do like one man, I can then begin to think about becoming exclusive with him.

The closest thing I've had to a relationship since joining S.L.A.A. was an awesome experience. After practicing for two years at being totally honest with women, it comes naturally to be totally honest with men.

That doesn't mean I share all. As with all the men I've dated since joining S.L.A.A., I focused on just being a friend. I was attracted to this man because of his emotional and spiritual maturity.

This was the first time in my life that I was developing a clean friendship with a man, not based on either of us using each other.

It was affirming to practice asking for what I needed, speaking my truth, and doing what was best for me despite his reaction. I was able to take baby steps forward to become close to him.

Because I went slowly, I was able to take baby steps backward when I needed to.

I decided to focus on only having sex after I got to know him well and was ready to deepen the relationship. I had found out earlier with another man that, when I set a time limit of when to have sex, I focused on the time and not, *Do I really like this person?*

I found it was best to stay in public places with him as we became more emotionally intimate.

In private places, I wanted to have sex with him. I noticed that, when we were in public, I didn't want him to touch me. It didn't take me long to see clearly, from my opposite feelings in public and private, that I would be using him for sex if I decided to get physically involved with him.

As time progressed, I was able to pinpoint why I didn't want him to touch me in public. There were certain behaviors that were physically unattractive to me.

Because he had these great spiritual and emotional qualities, I tried to talk myself into him being right for me. It was clear that I needed to accept him just the way he was and not try to change him.

As a human being, I am worthy of having a love relationship with a man who is not only emotionally and spiritually mature, but to whom I am physically attracted to also. I was trying to force things, thinking that as a spiritual person I should be able to rise above the physical thing. Meditation helped me accept the situation.

I am a human being, not God. For the first time in my life, I cleanly ended a relationship. He was wanting romance, and I was finally clear that I only wanted to be friends. I felt such dignity for myself. It was difficult for me to let go of him. At least it was something versus nothing. I was afraid I would slip back into a long withdrawal period.

It's been six weeks since I broke it off with him, and with affirmations and prayer I have not gone into withdrawal for more than a few hours at a time. Affirmations I use are: "I can trust God to guide me. I deserve a loving relationship. I celebrate my attraction to masculinity. I have the right to be selective."

I am making new male friends. I've had coffee and lunch with a few. I go into a little obsession once in a while. But otherwise, I am amazed at the miracles of this new way of life. It is a new lifestyle.

Today I celebrate the adventure of dating rather than recoiling with fear and mistrust. God is guiding me to Goodness.

— From *the Journal*, Issue #71

Questions:

1. What are your "stages of dating?"
2. Are there any tools that can help you enjoy the dating process more?
3. Do you feel more comfortable dating more than one person at a time or becoming exclusive fairly early? Discuss this with your sponsor or sober fellows who have gone through the dating process.
4. Write about the idea of focusing more on whether or not you like the person you are dating than on whether or not the person you are dating likes you.
5. Do you feel it's better for you to set a guideline of when to have sex in a relationship, or do you feel like the writer says, "when I set a time limit of when to have sex, I focused on the time and not, *Do I really like this person?*" Write about this and discuss with your sponsor.
6. Is there anything that your date does that you are overlooking because of their good qualities? Could overlooking these things eventually damage you or the relationship, or is it something that's okay to overlook?

STILL SIGNIFICANT

How often I've whined to my sponsor, my group, my "normal" friends, and even my cat that this is the longest I've ever been single in my entire adult life — four entire years. I've heard that there are people who've actually been celibate longer than I have. Notice that this addict interchanges single for celibate? Sometimes, I try to make a feeble joke of my singlehood. Surely, I've been celibate longer than the Pope! I've heard a few nuns get more action than I do! Please don't take this wrong. Such nonsense was never intended to offend anyone's religion. I have a fear of deprivation, of not getting enough attention, enough of anything and everything.

Ever since my addiction progressed to the point that it terrified me; I no longer arrange to meet women without first consulting my sponsor, and bookending the whole date process. With my sponsor's guidance, I have been doing the Internet dating thing. I have met all kinds of women, some interesting, a few slightly odd. And always, I pray to stay clear of my bottom-line danger zones.

The most important thing I have learned about my unprecedented Single Era: I am still a significant human being, whether or not a partner is in my life. I have used the opportunity to pursue a second career. I am attending graduate school part-time, which takes a lot of extra energy. Before S.L.A.A., I would have used all my energy to act out, to objectify women, to get a cheap hit. For the first time in this addict's life, I am learning to take a deep breath, be a little patient, and get to know a woman as another significant person. Maybe, together, if it is God's will, I will find my significant other. On the other hand, maybe I won't. Either way, I am a child of God. And, as always, He is taking care of me.

— From *the Journal*, Issue #107

Questions:

1. How do you deal with fear of deprivation?
2. How do you find patience?
3. Can you believe that Higher Power is taking care of you?

THERE IS NO BLAME

What I have come to discover from much work and many years in S.L.A.A. is that whatever has occurred in my life regarding personal relationships with the opposite sex has taken place because I was a participant!

Once I got this little insight, most of the anger and hurt I had been feeling regarding so-called "qualifiers" pretty much melted away. In all my relationships, I really am the common denominator! (And there's no "yeah, buts..."). I am an adult...I showed up for whatever the other person had to offer!!!

A self-parenting teacher told me years ago that all relationships are like a see-saw — if one person on the see-saw carries more weight than the other person, the see-saw will not be able to balance.

And that was pretty much my pattern of relationships before and even during my experience in S.L.A.A. I was willing to do "everything and anything" to make a relationship happen, yet I kept picking people who were barely able or willing to even show up. This in turn triggered enormous "family of origin" pain in me — gripping, paralyzing pain, and I did it over and over and over again.

It took me a long time to "get it," I mean, to really "get it," to truly value my own existence first before involving myself with another.

I am writing this in the hopes that possibly someone reading this will not continue to experience these same types of hurts and disappointments. If I can help another, the Third Step prayer says, then my victory over the pain, suffering and addiction has meaning.

I hear from sponsees and others of the terribly deep, intense pain and suffering that goes along in a situation with a potential or real partner not going the way we want it to go...for

97

example: "We had a few dates, (or a few months of dates), and he hasn't called."

What is the expectation on our part? And at least as important, what is the obligation on the part of the other person? He/she has *none.* Imposing expectations and obligations mean we are being hostage-takers.

I know we all want "love" but are we still going about receiving love in our old, addict-learned ways? If someone does not want to continue contact with you, it's important, vital, to go within and accept whatever feelings that may bring up, accept this moment in life, and let go of any expectation that this particular dating experience should carry any more weight than "an experience."

This is one reason why it's so crucial not to get physical before knowing the person. And 10 dates do not add up to "knowing" someone. I hear over and over again in meetings how people date for a few weeks, then suddenly they are "in a relationship." They are "in bliss."

Then they come back to the meeting a few weeks, months later, and talk about how much trouble and pain the relationship/other person is creating. But that is *our* doing...once again we created a "love" situation without learning enough about the other person first.

It takes time to fully experience another person. But, in three- or six-weeks-time, if there is physical attraction, all we can know is our fantasy of who we hope, wish and pray that person will be.

We don't have the necessary experience and information about the other person to move into the sexual realm, and people so often do, and cause themselves so much grief and pain and heartache, and then, as we say in our "Characteristics of Sex and Love Addiction," blame them for not fulfilling our fantasies and expectations.

It is vital for us as recovering addicts to take care of our emotions, our feelings, our hearts, our bodies, before involving ourselves with someone else. We do need to "become responsible for ourselves before involving ourselves with others," even when the need to bond and give and receive love is so great and strong and primal.

I never knew before coming to S.L.A.A. and other 12-Step programs that there could be so much joy and fulfillment in discovering who I am, completely separate from others.

What are my values, my interests, my tastes, my passions? The way I grew up was so much about taking care of others, pleasing others (to "get" love...which didn't really work even then!) that I did not know these things about myself and perhaps even worse, didn't know how to value me.

Through lots of years of hard work, and showing up, I am able to feel and acknowledge the value of myself.

— From the Journal, Issue #137

Questions:

1. The article says, "...all relationships are like a see-saw — if one person on the see-saw carries more weight than the other person, the see-saw will not be able to balance." How do you maintain balance in a relationship?
2. How do you feel you can help another in S.L.A.A.?
3. How do you deal with unrealistic expectations and unmet realistic expectations?
4. How do you react when a date isn't calling you back?

LIVING A COMPLETELY DIFFERENT LIFE

Being in S.L.A.A. has completely changed my life. Actually, I think it would be more accurate to say that being in S.L.A.A. has *given* me a life.

Before recovery, I had no life. It may have looked like I had a life, but what I was doing was just "borrowing" a life from whatever guy I was with. His hobbies would become my hobbies. His interests would become my interests. And his friends would become my friends.

But none of these things were mine. And when the relationship ended, I'd have to "borrow" a life from the next guy. Then I'd get a completely different set of hobbies, friends and interests. On my own, I was like a hollow shell. I had no idea what I liked or who I was.

When I entered withdrawal in S.L.A.A., I had to face the fact that without a guy around, my world was pretty empty. I felt so lonely and isolated. I had nothing and no one in my life to fill the void. I desperately needed to come up with some top-line behaviors if I was going to make it. But I had no idea where to start. I couldn't think of anything. I was at a complete loss when it came to taking care of myself or having fun.

So, I started listening for suggestions from my fellows, picking up ideas from the shares that I'd hear in meetings. I started making a list.

In the beginning, the top lines on my list were very simple. Take a bath. Go for a walk. Pick up the phone and call a fellow. During one of my first outreach calls, when I was deep in withdrawal and wanting to act out, a long timer suggested that I call a friend and ask to meet for coffee. I was too ashamed to tell her that I didn't have any friends. But I added her suggestion to the list.

As time went on, the list got longer, and I would refer to it whenever I was feeling triggered and needed something positive to fill my time. Even something as simple as petting my cat or eating something nutritious could help. I started adding more things to the list that could help me out of my anorexia and isolation, beginning with very simple actions like getting out of bed when the alarm goes off in the morning.

Eventually, I added more challenging things like taking a class or volunteering. I kept adding to the list. Go to a play. Visit a museum. Go to the beach. Try something new. I knew I really needed to connect with other people, and so I'd try to do some of these things with someone else. Invite someone to go to a play. But sometimes that was just too scary. And that had to be okay. It had to be about progress, not perfection. Going to a museum by myself was better than not going at all.

With time and practice, top-line actions got easier and easier. Some of them just became good habits, like making my bed and washing my dishes. I eventually found myself actually making friends of my own, saying yes to more invitations and reaching out more.

I started having fun! I discovered that I love swing dancing, and I now go dancing every Thursday. I joined a group of program friends in forming a "movie club" going to dinner and a movie every weekend.

Slowly and gradually, I was developing a life of my own. And all the while, I was also working my program, sticking to my bottom lines, going to meetings, working the steps with my sponsor, being of service, and building a relationship with a Higher Power.

After about two years in program, with the help of my sponsor, I developed a dating plan and began "sober dating" while also maintaining my commitment to my program and to my own life. Today, after 3½ years in S.L.A.A., I'm now in my first "sober" healthy relationship with a great guy. For now, I only see him twice a week, and the rest of the time I continue living my own life.

A few weeks ago, my boyfriend left for a month-long trip abroad with his daughter. Based on my past history, I was a little nervous about how I would handle this time alone and what my life would look like in his absence. I quickly realized, though, just how much all that hard work of developing and maintaining top lines had paid off, and just how very rich and full my life is today.

Literally every single day since he's been gone (except for Tuesdays, when I have my acting class), someone has invited me to do something fun. One friend had an extra concert ticket. Then another friend invited me to dinner. Then a group of us went to see Shakespeare in the park. Then I went to a movie. How very, very different my life is today, compared to that bleak and empty place that I was trying to fill with "borrowed" lives. I am no longer lonely and isolated. Today my life is fun and rich and full, even when there's no guy around!

— From the Journal, Issue #163

Questions:

1. Do you have friends that you socialize with outside of your dating or relationship? How often do you go out alone or with friends?
2. List your top line behaviors.
3. How do you maintain balance in your life? Is this difficult during dating?

4. List any character defects that stand in the way of maintaining top line behaviors.

Defect	How it affects my ability to engage in top line behavior
Self-centered fear	*Don't want to call people because they might hurt me*
Fear of rejection	*Refuse to open up to people*

Do a fear and resentment inventory on each.

5. List fears that come up whenever a partner goes out of town or is unavailable. What can you do to lessen these fears?

DATING – LETTING GO OF ANTICIPATION

When I started dating, I had to use all the tools of the Program, as the dynamics of online dating are so similar to the hookup apps that had brought me to my knees with obsession, mania and despair. If I am going to survive dating, I am going to need help. I literally do not have a clue about what I'm doing, and the pitfalls are many. I also really want to control the outcome, as in I need a life partner – NOW! So, having no clue and full speed ahead is surely a recipe for disaster once again. One good thing about recovery is that the inherent introspection and honesty teaches me to recognize when I need help. The stakes are so high around finding a healthy compatible life partner, that I definitely need help from my Higher Power and others in the program. So, as I got on the dating sites, I adopted an attitude of letting go of outcomes, of not letting anything that happens disturb me, so my serenity stays intact. The dynamics of the dating sites are so much like it was on the hookup sites - I text them...why aren't they responding? Wait...they just read my text...why aren't they responding? What are they hiding?

Why am I not important? The anticipation is starting to make me manic. I like what they said in their profile... they are very attractive.... Damn it, I'm starting to pick out drapes...why aren't they responding?! This needs to happen! I need to meet them! Will they like the color of the drapes?... and down the rabbit hole of obsession I go once again.

Once I recognized the insanity of the anticipation angst, I embraced an approach of surrendering it all to God.

So now I message them, then let it go. I don't let the thoughts get going of what a cute couple we would be. So, I have taken a matter of fact, surrendered approach to online dating. I message them in a sane friendly way, then let go of the outcome. I don't let myself get swept up and intoxicated by the anticipation. I take the attitude of, "if they respond to me-good. If they don't, maybe it wasn't meant to be." It is all up to God anyway. These people popped up on my screen because it was God's will. So, if I make myself crazy with anticipation, that would obviously not be God's will. That is me making myself manic by once again trying to control the uncontrollable.

In many respects, the creation of that so called "killer" dating profile is all about my will and pride. I was driven to create the perfect profile – pick out the perfect photos. Notice that word "driven," not inspired. When I have so much self-will and pride wrapped up in something, I've learned it just ends up making me crazy. So, I'm letting go. God is the director of this dating game. I'm happy to let him work his magic. It is going to be good. It always is when my Higher Power runs the show.

— From the Journal, Issue #166

Questions:

1. What are some dating pitfalls for you?
2. Do you do online dating? List the pros and cons of this method of dating for you.
3. How do you maintain serenity while dating?
4. How do or can you let go of outcomes in dating? Do you surrender your will or keep taking back control? If you can't surrender, how can you become more willing?
5. How do you deal with anticipation?
6. How do you tell the difference between God's will and your will in dating? Give examples from past dating experiences.

FIRST THINGS FIRST

These are the strategies I have used for staying sober and determining behaviors for my bottom line. It includes how I deal with desires to act out and lack of clarity in decision-making. When my sponsor and I started our relationship three years ago, I had 2-1/2 years sobriety and ten behaviors that made up my bottom line. The first thing that she asked me to tell her was what my behaviors on my bottom line were and why they were there. My bottom line included no sex outside a committed relationship, or before three months into a relationship, and no intimate relationships at the workplace or at my 12-Step meetings because I wanted to keep these places safe. She suggested that I take the behavior of masturbating while sleeping off of my bottom line, since I was not conscious when this was happening.

Interestingly enough, I had just added a new bottom line behavior a week before finding my sponsor and that was not to return to past partners to protect my supply. I have been known to return to a partner twenty years later as part of keeping my addiction alive.

Little did I realize, that within a few months of adding that bottom line, my three-year relationship would end. Luckily, my sponsor and I discussed my reasons for letting the relationship go and I felt I had made an adult decision without the guilt and shame. I was in recovery!

After six months out of the relationship, my sponsor suggested I make a list of what I wanted in a relationship and in a person before I started dating again. I realized that I wanted someone plus or minus five years of my own age, medication-free, non-smoker, emotionally and physically available and independent, (not only financially, but also professionally and personally).

Then it hit me that I had never dated before. I mean, whenever I went out with someone, I went right to bed and had sex (if not on the first date, then most certainly shortly thereafter). I had not seen the benefit in getting to know someone first. But at the age of 56, without a partner and a string of unsuccessful partnerships, I became teachable.

Many discussions about how an older lesbian could meet other older lesbians, besides in bars or at 12-Step meetings, ensued before I decided that Internet dating might be feasible. As I began Internet dating, one of my first reactions was an intense desire to return to the relationship I had just left. The yearning was so strong that it was all I could do to call my sponsor instead of my past lover. My sponsor then introduced to me a process that I could use in most situations, whether changing my bottom line or doing something difficult. What my sponsor suggested was the following:

- List the Pros/Cons.
  Example: If I contact her, what are the positives and negatives to that action?
- Identify my motives.
  Example: Why do I want to take this action?
- Determine my expectations.
  Example: What do I expect to get from this action?
- Itemize my fears.
  Example: What am I afraid of right now, related to this action and in general?
- Consider the consequences.
  Example: What can happen because of this action?

Considering all the answers to the five previous items, can I live with the consequences? Are my expectations reasonable? Am I trying to avoid a fear?

After doing this written exercise, I called my sponsor to

discuss what I had learned about myself. I was instructed to wait twenty-four hours, breathe, and pray. This gave my Higher Power a chance to reveal to me anything else. The fact is that, by following these suggestions, I did not act out or interrupt my sobriety or make an unhealthy choice.

I continued dating and met many women over six-months within a five-hour drive of my home. The strategy used to date by Internet was to email a few times, give my phone number, and then recommend a first date over coffee or lunch. All this occurred within a few weeks of the first contact. The first date would be during the day, somewhere halfway between where we both lived.

I dated two women seriously and committed to one. Then the horrible day came when I had my first slip in S.L.A.A. after four years of sobriety. I had sex at nine weeks, just over two months into the relationship instead of considering sexual intimacy only after three months.

I did not use the process that worked so well for other choices. I wanted to fire my sponsor, quit the S.L.A.A. program and just do A.A.

When I wanted to drink after ten years of sobriety from alcohol, I knew I had to recommit to both 12-Step programs and to all my bottom- line behaviors.

After my slip, my sponsor suggested I call her daily, which I did for ten days and then twice a week. I also committed to going to at least two S.L.A.A. meetings per week. My sponsor also suggested that every day I should write about one of the questions from the pamphlet, "40 Questions for Self-Diagnosis."

This resulted in my adding three new bottom line behaviors:

1. No dating anyone more than an hour's drive away.

2. No overnight dating.

3. No sex for six months in a new committed relationship. I also have recommitted to using the process described earlier to

109

help me make informed choices and decisions. One of the greatest gifts of recovery and sobriety in the 12-Step program is to pass it on; to pass on the tools and things that work, that help me stay sober and help me help others.

As my sponsor said, if I do not know the behaviors that form my bottom line, or if my sponsees do not know their bottom line behaviors, we are not able to work the Steps, especially Step 1, because we do not know what we are powerless over. After all, it is about first things first! Once I identify those behaviors, I am responsible for keeping the commitments to myself and using these tools that I have outlined. I am no longer a victim of my addiction.

— From the Journal, Issue #98

Questions:

1. Do regrets from past relationships or longing to return to past relationships crop up when you are dating? If they do, what do you do about them? Write about the desire to contact an ex using the outline presented in this article (list the pros and cons, identify motives, determine expectations, itemize fears, consider the consequences).

MY MOST IMPORTANT BOTTOM LINES

I was told to make a list of the things that triggered the insanity that brought me to my knees around my sex and love addiction.

And fortunately for me it was very clear what I did. The wildest and most wicked thing I did centered in desire and fantasy and frequently led to my destruction.

I would fall hook, line, and sinker for a man I barely even knew. I'd think I was head over heels in love and that he was head over heels in love with me too when we'd just barely met.

It began with a life-long desire to be loved totally and completely. My parents were supposed to fill this need from my first breath but unfortunately, they never did.

It was thwarted love. I had a loving, kind, and caring dad but my mom and brothers were all very abusive to me. My mother was both verbally and physically abusive to me. Both of my brothers sexually abused me.

My mom was a rage-aholic who seemed to get a greater thrill from tormenting me than she did from my brothers. So, in the end I just wanted to be loved. That was all. The problem was that I confused a lot of things with love.

The second part of the problem was fantasy, fairy tale fantasy to be precise. I wanted to be loved and really believed that there was a perfect person out there for me who was going to sweep me off my feet and take all my problems away. We were going to be so totally and completely in love that nothing could ever shake us.

I could do no wrong towards him and he would never do any wrong towards me.

We would have plenty of money to live in a nice home, travel the world and experience a great life together. Ha!

The combo of intense desire and fantasy led me to

heartbreak after heartbreak and I just thought something was terribly wrong with me.

Of course, no one could ever fulfill all the huge expectations I had! It felt like my very own mother didn't love me so there just must have been something unlovable about me. And I couldn't figure out what it was.

So, one of the first and most liberating bottom lines I've set so far in my 4 ½ years of sobriety is, I do not allow myself to fall head over heels for someone.

I take my time to get to know someone for who they really are, not for who I fantasize them to be.

I don't ever do the "He's the One" drama with someone I'm dating anymore.

I cannot entertain that kind of diseased thinking.

Instead I ask myself, "Is he the one I want to go out on one more date with?" Or "Is he the one I want to be my boyfriend for one more day?"

I can't tell you how miraculous this bottom line has been for me. It sounds simple but the application of it is very difficult.

I must watch myself like a hawk because I'll project what is happening today to what might or could happen in the future and then I realize I'm on the fast track to my demise.

I pray the 3rd Step Prayer and change my focus immediately.

One of the many beautiful things about this is that it has forced me to slow down my dating process a lot. And while my addict doesn't like that, the new healthy me loves it.

There's no rush.

I don't need the hit of approval I used to thrive on. I no longer need all the drama this downward spiral of insanity used to bring to my life.

I'm no longer looking for a super-hero or a knight in shining armor. I'm just looking for a real, fallible man just like me, (a real, fallible woman) to get to know and see if we want to spend more time together. That's all.

The second most powerful bottom line I've set so far is what I call my 30-day or 10 date dating manifesto. For no less than 30 days or 10, 2-or-more-hour dates, no clothing comes off! And what that means to me is that I do not sexualize myself or my date in any way for 30 or more days or 10 or more dates. Nothing sexual is said or done.

This supports me in getting to know him for who he really is, not for just how sexually compatible we are and it helps him to get to know me for who I am and not just for my sensuousness and sexuality.

I've had to create an ironclad dating plan to enforce this and it works like magic, but it is not easy at all! And it's not perfect.

My date might say something sexual or overly flirty with me and the old me would quickly crank it up a notch or two, but my healthy new self can respond slowly and calmly and dial it down instead of crank it up!

The dating plan that helps me achieve this, and I've done so in two sober, committed and monogamous relationships so far, helps me achieve the kind of pace that keeps me sober, calm and level-headed.

It allows no sexual fantasizing about my date. This is a big one for me. How could I ever keep my pants zipped if I was getting myself all worked up fantasizing about a guy? Another method to my dating madness was an extremely romantic playlist I had that I would listen to all the time, song after romantic and sexual song! No more.

These two were the big triggering kingpins for me. Identifying these and setting bottom lines around them transformed my life.

There are a lot more details to the dating plan but honestly my 30-day, or 10 date, dating manifesto, eliminating fantasizing and eliminating extremely romantic and sexual music from my life has given me so much peace in dating that it is amazing.

The most important thing about these bottom lines is that they have given me freedom!

I am free to learn how to have real, healthy, happy relationships and I'm very happy to say that I'm getting better and better at it all the time.

I'm getting better at picking the men who are good for me instead of the ones who trigger my wild and wicked insanity.

I am so very thankful for all the men and women who share about their bottom lines, dating plans and about their relationships in our meetings and on outreach calls. There is so much hope available to us in S.L.A.A. but we must work the Steps and do everything within our power to lead serene and sober lives.

While the sober relationship I'm in now is still new, I'm seeing behaviors in me I never thought possible before.

When the old me wants to say or do something that's not so healthy, I see it now ahead of time and I stop and smile to myself in gratitude that my disease no longer runs me.

— From the Journal, Issue #164

Questions:

1. How do you stay out of obsessive fantasy?
2. How do you deal with a person you are dating who moves too fast?
3. Do romantic songs trigger you? What do you do about it?

HIGHS AND LOWS OF SOBER DATING

Hello, I am MP, a low bottom sex addict who through the grace of a Higher Power, has come to enjoy the highs and lows of that dreaded catch phrase "sober dating!"

Now, I can tell you that there was a time I would have laughed in your face if you told me I would one day be happily sharing coffee for one hour with complete strangers with no physical contact, intriguing or propositioning.

The very thought of that was alternatingly mind-numbingly boring, or nauseating, or both.

I can remember being asked on a date once and saying, "No," at which point the guy asked me if I wanted to have a one-night stand. Within a week, I was pregnant.

And that was how most attempts at dating went for me, sadly. Sometimes I would try to date people after we'd had sex. That was a sad scene indeed.

There was nothing to talk about, as we had already accelerated the relationship to its demise, sometimes within a mere 24 hours. So, the first thing to absorb about sober dating is that the rate of getting to know someone is quite slow. In movies, the characters must progress through their love affairs within two hours or less, and this fantasy world has subtly influenced our ideas about relationships.

In real life, two hours is an extremely short amount of time to know someone. It's like two seconds.

It takes weeks and months to get a fuller picture of an individual in terms of their values, lifestyle and personality and to account for the fact that most people show themselves at their very best at first, gradually becoming their more ordinary selves over time.

Thinking back to my very first sober date, I was petrified. I went to a meeting beforehand and was just sweating bricks.

I felt I was going to the guillotine. "In fear for my life" as they say.

The date went fine, the guy was much shorter and smaller than his picture, but very nice and kind. After that it got easier. I went on about 25 first dates, and then met my ex-boyfriend.

He was late to the first date. I brushed it aside, because he was very sexy.

He also chose a restaurant that had nothing on the menu I could eat. This too I brushed aside.

Before I knew it, I was in a full pattern of not expressing my true needs and wants. I was being inauthentic.

But I was just so relieved someone finally wanted me. I had the feeling I should keep sober dating, but I was too lazy and tired, and I wanted to get the accolades of what I felt would come to me if I was "successful" in S.L.A.A. at getting a relationship.

So, within a few weeks, he had asked me to be his girlfriend. I cut the sober dating process short and proceeded into the relationship. Six months later I was back in withdrawal, shaking my head.

So, I learned the hard way that sober dating will test me along the way to take shortcuts through the process — to get off the sober dating train early and try to nest up with someone rather than continue the endless awkwardness.

A word about awkwardness. I can tell you, during one of my first sober dates, I once brought up an article I had just read about prison rape. Somehow, I thought that was a good topic to discuss on a first date with a man.

I've also gone on dates and discussed child abuse, or topics like being born in a cult. Today I keep it "light and bright" on the date. I talk about puppies, or movies, or food, or even puppies in movies eating food, but I keep the dark, death metal side of me in the wings.

116

I do not discuss my exes, or my toxic family, or politics, or anything (including how much I hate Hans Zimmer because there are so many other overlooked film composers) that brings stress or excess depth.

First dates are meant to be fun. I usually try to schedule them for coffee, or sometimes with an activity like ping pong or air hockey (something that keeps me in the shallow end of the pool). I had to read "Small Talk for Dummies" and learn how to discuss the weather. I've discovered that small talk is very useful, and it has a place in my life. I've also learned that first dates should be fairly short, no more than one hour. For me, that is a way of expressing gentleness and not overwhelming myself or the other person.

Also, in recovery, I've come to let men pay for me on dates. Not sure why, but I used to get a huge thrill from denying them the chance to do that, and proving I could pay for myself, or that I don't need a man to take care of me.

The truth is, it feels kind of sweet to have the check picked up, and as old fashioned as it is, I am okay with some of these gendered dating rituals. I just say thank you, rather than trying to start a feminist riot on every date.

As for encountering active sex and love addicts on dates, wow that's a tough one. I've recently had a guy ask me back to his place after our first date and I got so triggered I had to go to bed at 8:30 p.m. on a Saturday night to keep from acting out.

But over that long sleep, I realized that my 12th Step work doesn't stop just because I'm on a date. I was able to email that young man and tell him I was in program and express powerlessness to him. He thanked me and apologized for being so aggressive. To me, that is a miracle. That I could stay sober, that I could be honest, that I could share the solution, those are huge gifts to me, a low bottom sex addict who is beyond human aid.

At any rate, I am still sober dating, learning more about myself each day and continuing to say the Set Aside Prayer:

"Dear God, please help me to set aside everything I think I know about dating, romance, sex, love, intimacy and relationships so I may have an open mind and a new experience. Please help me to see the truth about myself and my dating partners. AMEN."

If you're reading this and just starting your sober dating process, I wish you great courage, self-love and patience. We in the program are right here with you, supporting you and smiling at you from afar. We know the bravery it takes to step back into the ring with the tiger. But one day at a time, tigers are growing into very fine ladies and gentlemen of honor and integrity. It's happening right before our eyes. Higher Power is stretching our hearts and minds and no doubt has a hand in all our affairs. Good luck!

— From the Journal, Issue #165

Questions:

1. What happened when you moved too fast while dating (if you did)? Was the relationship salvageable? Write about this.
2. Do you ignore red flags during dates?
3. What happens if you take shortcuts in the dating process?
4. Are there topics that you feel you should avoid while on a date?
5. How do you/would you handle encountering an active sex and love addict on a date?
6. Can you feel confident that your Twelve-Step work and Higher Power can keep you safe?

ALL I WANT IS A GPS RELATIONSHIP!

Dating sucks! I've been on almost every dating website out there. (Although, I'm very proud to say I never went on any of the shadier websites. But that's precisely what my sex and love addiction wants me to do.)

Once I got into the program, I settled into eHarmony. It seemed to have the least amount of insanity involved and it seemed to trigger my addiction the least.

Nevertheless, it is challenging. After tons of first dates that were not followed by a second, I've come to one conclusion: No more OMG chemistry that leads to WTF relationships and tons of SOS calls to my sponsor and recovery partners! No more!

Now, all I'm looking for is GPS chemistry that leads me to a Graceful, Peaceful and Serene relationship with a quality man.

With GPS chemistry, I'm still attracted to the man, but not so much that I want to leap over the table and into his lap while he's still buttering his bread.

OMG chemistry is crazy-making and sets me completely off balance to the point where I can't even sleep at night because I'm thinking about him so much.

It usually triggers all the magical thinking that I have to work hard in my recovery to avoid.

GPS chemistry is self-loving. It gives me the ability to honor my #1 bottom line for dating: To stay grounded in reality and in my own life.

GPS chemistry is calming and stable. It allows me to continue to work my program, live my life to its fullest and still look forward to the next date.

GPS chemistry truly guides me in the direction that is best for me instead of me getting lost in the insanity of dating.

How much chemistry there is between me and someone I'm dating plays a significant role in my recovery.

119

OMG chemistry does not support me in my recovery. It is very distracting.

GPS chemistry empowers me to be the best woman I can be and to act like a lady so that I can attract the best man for me in my recovery.

Ultimately my Higher Power is in charge of this GPS chemistry instead of me. With this kind of chemistry, it is easy for me to stay connected and let my Higher Power guide me.

It is easy for me to surrender my will and my life when the relationship begins with chemistry that is graceful, peaceful,l and serene.

— From the Journal, Issue #146

Questions:

1. How do you maintain sobriety when confronted with dramatic chemistry while dating? What thoughts crop up when you have bland chemistry with your date? Write about any fears that come up.
2. How do you stay grounded in reality while dating?
3. Do you look forward to dates or do you dread them? How do you deal with anorexia?

CHOICE

I meet a man. A traveler. A thinker. A seeker. He meets me. A shining, brilliant, funny woman.

I have been celibate and in S.L.A.A. for a year and a half; I am beginning to date for the first time. Ever. The jasmine breeze and the sun's heat awaken my body, my mind. I am alive to my sense of myself in connection with spirit. I am in touch with my true strength, committed to the practices that center me, expand my consciousness, allow me to accept change and expand my skills as an effective instrument of my highest self.

This man pursues a connection with me, and I allow myself to be open, curious, and adventurous with him. I allow myself to experience and express feelings, dreams, passions, and my vulnerabilities with him. I choose which thoughts to express, which stories I want to reaffirm about who I am, and which I am ready to release. I let go of old defense mechanisms that get in the way of human experience.

We proceed at a gentle pace, both of us patient and confident that events are unfolding organically. I tell him that I really like him, and that I really like the person who likes him.

I allow this man to express interest in me, to appreciate me, to give to me, to know me, to come to care for me. I observe the pull toward the old ways, and reaffirm to God, to myself, and to my close friends that I am ready to move forward, into the unknown. I will no longer believe I am not good enough to be loved. I waver and learn to right myself and learn that this continuing process is part of life. I courageously and triumphantly endure fierce trials of silence, of space, of attacks from my own mind. I remain gracious, clear, and, above all, I remain inside the faith that what I desire, which is aligned with Spirit, is on its way. There is nothing for me to worry about. I sing a song of gratitude.

121

Both of us have been on a healing path, and we tread on new, sober terrain, building a sustainable foundation based on friendship, instead of a shaky foundation based solely on sexual connection. We choose not to even kiss yet.

We practice communicating, dancing, sharing, and exploring new things together.

I discover connection, equality, and attraction at physical, emotional, political, familial, intellectual, contextual, and spiritual levels. We bathe in our light for God and for one another. We experience bliss staring into one another's eyes. We meet one another's friends. We chose to be monogamous with one another, to only explore this special kind of friendship and relationship with each other.

During this process, I continue to live my life, to be with friends, to perform, to write, to make a living, to pursue my life's purpose, and to find love, intimacy, and care within my communities, apart from him. I give of myself, of my heart, share my home and my bed cuddling and holding one another, share cherished and meaningful music and poetry with him, and receive his gifts with open arms. I recognize in myself the tender, sexy, powerful, beautiful, whole, wise and humble woman I've always known myself to be. Knowing him inspires me to take risks to expand my universe, to learn new things, to keep my house in order to be available to myself and to him and to God, to be present, to cultivate gratitude for the gifts I am continually receiving and take them as a sign of God's love.

Upon an unexpected period of extended reflection, this man realizes he is simply not ready for partnership. I see that I have chosen to open my heart to a kind, conscientious man. He gathers his resources to clearly, calmly, carefully, gently, and respectfully explain the context for this change. I gather my resources, surround myself with loving women, men, and spirits — mourn this shift in expectations, celebrate the profound and tender nature of human ability to love, and grow to accept that change is the only constant. I dwell in the heart of my sweet Lord, whose divine plan for me is abundant, fulfilling, and meaningful beyond my wildest dreams.

— From the Journal, Issue #105

Questions:

1. What practices: A) center you, B) expand your consciousness, C) allow you to accept change, and D) expand your skills as an instrument of your highest self while dating?

2. How do you keep balance in dealing with your sex and love addiction while trying to be open, curious, and adventurous? Are there fears that hold you back from being open, curious, and adventurous? Are these healthy fears or anorexia?

3. Is there anything that blocks you from expressing feelings, dreams, passions, and vulnerabilities to partners? If so, is it healthy to have a time frame while dating before you reveal certain things? How long before it becomes anorexia?

4. Do you feel confident in your power to choose? If not, write about this and discuss it with your sponsor. Say a prayer for Higher Power's guidance.

5. What are your old defense mechanisms that get in the way of human experience?

6. Make a gratitude list about dating.

7. How do you maintain the belief that Higher Power has a plan for your life when faced with rejection?

DATING IN THE FREEDOM OF SOBRIETY

I am very grateful for the S.L.A.A. program. In the last two months, I have had 5 sober dates with a guy I met through someone I know.

The first week, I was feeling soooooo in love, sure we would get married, etc. Then, some days later I was expecting his call and I fell into my "I am not loved, not lovable" hole and lived a big lot of drama, a lot of suffering and emotional crisis.

I talked about it for hours with my sponsor and my S.L.A.A. friends and wrote in my journal a lot. After a little while, I started to "detach" and went to the "I don't care about him (damn him)" end.

My sponsor helped me see I was not angry about him, but about my past wounds and patterns, that this guy was just living his life. And that it was a good sign that he wouldn't stop his life to jump into mine... He finally called and we had some other dates, slowly getting to know each other.

What I want to share is the miracle now happening. In the last week, I have strengthened my spiritual practices and received the grace of feeling that I am enough, I am loved. You know, what they say, "The love of God flowing through oneself." I felt it.

I saw that of course I will have a boyfriend at some point, because that happens in people's lives, it's normal, it's legitimate. I don't have to take whatever is passing by, as if I didn't deserve anything good.

I can relax and see if a guy is a good fit for me, not try to make things work because it would be my last chance.

I don't need to have a boyfriend. It will certainly be fun and an enrichment in my life. (And also, a lot of spiritual and emotional work to stay centered!) But I don't need a boyfriend because the source of love is in my connection with my Higher

Power, not in a boyfriend. Actually, I usually feel worse with a boyfriend since I project on them my self-hatred and attack them for "making me feel so bad."

The grace I received in the last few months was to see to what extent the pain and suffering is INSIDE ME, not caused by the other person. So, loving myself and turning my will and my life over to a Higher Power of infinite love, I don't have to look for love outside.

So, I may or may not become intimate with that guy. I don't know. I don't have to know. I don't have to control, nor do I have to make things happen. I don't have to analyze it all and worry. I can just live my wonderful life, take great care of myself, work my one day at a time program and enjoy the blessings in my life. More will be revealed in the right time. And the miracle is that I FEEL IT very deeply, I LIVE it today! Wow!

All this is pretty new, and I know my path won't be perfect forever after. But I am so grateful for what I've heard in program since my first meetings almost eight years ago.

That gives me hope of a true sobriety, an emotional sobriety.

I have to admit that I don't quite know what having a boyfriend is for if it is not to make me feel good. How do I relate if I don't spend my time expecting, then blaming, making crisis and drama, demanding attention, creating deep talks about emotions because I crave connection...?

After I found sobriety in my behavior, I am discovering the sobriety of mind and emotions. I am grateful because thanks to S.L.A.A., I can write about my sick behavior and lovingly laugh at myself. It is okay that I don't know how to act in a different way.

The only thing I have to do is be open and willing to learn a new way, listening to members that have what I want, and most of all nourishing my connection with this almighty Higher Power that IS the source of love.

Questions:

1. Have you ever realized that anger at a person you were dating was really just past wounds and patterns? If so, describe the triggers and the events from the past that came up. How did you react? Did you make amends?
2. Write about the idea that it's a good sign when a date doesn't stop their life in order to jump into your life.
3. Do you feel a partner is necessary for your life? If so, why? If not, why not?

A SOBER DATING PLAN HELPS ME RECOGNIZE UNAVAILABILITY

Thank God for my sober dating plan! I don't know how else I could possibly stand a chance of being able to recognize when someone is unavailable. Following my dating plan gives me the time and space that I need to be able to see clearly.

When I dated prior to S.L.A.A. recovery, I would plunge ahead so fast, with my sight so focused on the fantasy of who this person was or what this relationship was supposed to be, that I was literally blind to the reality of who they actually were. If information surfaced that didn't fit with my plans, I'd just disregard it, rationalize it, or explain it away. He's got a girlfriend? Yeah, but their relationship is on the rocks. He's not interested in a long-term relationship? Yeah, but he's only saying that because he's been hurt before. He just took a job that's transferring him out of the country? Yeah, well, it's not like that's set in stone. And if I was able to ignore these really big signs of unavailability, then there was no way I was ever even going to notice the smaller, more subtle ones.

When I follow my dating plan, on the other hand, the amount of time that I spend with someone is very limited. I'm forced to go very, very slowly. In the beginning, I don't see someone more than once a week, and I don't talk or text with them more than what's necessary to set up the next date. So, there's a lot of space in between dates. That space is the key, I have found. It allows time for that post-date (or pre-date) excitement, the "high" of the fantasy, to fade. And then I get to look at the reality.

The reality is, how is this person actually showing up for me? Even before the first date, is it hard for me to get them to commit to a specific time and place? Are they willing to make advance plans? (My dating plan requires at least 3 days' notice.)

129

Do they return my text/call in a timely fashion? And on the date, do they seem to be present? Are they listening? Do they have good boundaries, not over-sharing or talking all about their past relationships? I have found that I can't really get clarity around these questions without that space.

I'll share one of my early sober dating experiences as an example. I went on several dates with this guy whom I'd been interested in for some time. He was sweet and funny, and there seemed to be some chemistry.

There were a couple of moments where I wasn't really sure if he was truly listening to me, but they weren't enough to keep me from making another date with him. I liked him. I told myself that he was probably just nervous.

We went on several very nice dates. And he made it clear that he was really into me. But in that space in between the dates, I couldn't quite shake the sense that he just wasn't quite present, that he wasn't really seeing me.

Now, I can PROMISE you, without my dating plan, I would have absolutely plunged ahead. I wouldn't have taken that space. I would have stayed in the fog of the post-date "high," extending it from one date to the next by staying in constant contact with him, texting, calling, checking his social media, etc. I also would have plunged ahead into physical intimacy, getting drunk on the chemistry, which of course only thickens that blinding fog. In the end, I had to conclude that even though he was really pursuing me, he just wasn't emotionally available for the kind of true connection that I'm looking for.

Having been through a few situations like this now, it's pretty clear to me that I absolutely WOULD NOT have been able to recognize this guy's unavailability without the time and space that my dating plan affords me. However, when I *do* give myself that time and space, I have found that it becomes almost easy to spot those signs. I've also found that it gets easier with practice.

That's not to say, though, that taking the space isn't hard as hell. It is. I couldn't possibly do it without constant contact with my sponsor, my fellows and especially my Higher Power, every step of the way. Following my dating plan is a spiritual experience. It requires that I am constantly turning my will and my life over to my Higher Power. Just like with my bottom lines, I try not to think of my dating plan as a set of "rules" that I must obey. I think of it as a set of guidelines, the purpose of which is surrender, to help me to stay out of my own will. And if I can just stay out of my own will, my Higher Power can reveal to me everything I need to see.

— From the Journal, Issue # 167

Questions:

1. How do you recognize when someone is unavailable?
2. Describe times you disregarded, rationalized, or explained away information that didn't fit with your plans for dating or relationships. How do you avoid this in sobriety?
3. Describe a time, if any, that you realized you were with an unavailable person. What did you do about it? Where did you find support? What would you do if you encountered someone unavailable now?
4. Do you agree that following a dating plan is a spiritual experience? Why or why not?

Part IV – Summary & Meeting Resources

After the reading and answering questions:

Dating Checklist

(check all of the commitments you are willing to make)

___ I will make/continue a dating plan

___ I will go to _____ meetings per week while dating

___ I will pray and meditate

___ I will get/continue hobbies (list:)

_____

___ I will engage in self-care (list:)

_____

___ I will maintain relationships with my friends, sponsor, family, and Higher Power

___ I will take care of my responsibilities

___ I will bookend dates with sponsor or trusted fellows

___ I will work on my character defects

___ I will stay out of fantasy

___ I will be present on dates to the best of my ability

___ I will be self-supporting through my own contributions

___ I will be open and honest with people I date, myself and fellows

___ I am willing to believe Higher Power has a plan for my dating life

___ I will listen and be of service while dating

___ I will be kind to and forgiving of myself

___ I will have fun dating

Sober Dating: Questions for Discussion Meeting Format

Welcome to the Sober Dating: Questions for Discussion Meeting of Sex and Love Addicts Anonymous.

My name is_____ and I am a sex and love addict and the leader for this meeting. Will you please join me in the Serenity Prayer?

God, grant me the serenity to accept the things I cannot change, courage to change the things I can, and the wisdom to know the difference.

Sex and Love Addicts Anonymous is a Twelve Step, Twelve Tradition oriented fellowship based on the model pioneered by Alcoholics Anonymous.

The only requirement for S.L.A.A. membership is a desire to stop living out a pattern of sex and love addiction. S.L.A.A. is supported entirely through the contributions of its membership and is free to all who need it.

At this time, we will read from the "Sober Dating: Questions for Discussion" book.

This week we will begin reading _____. We will do a round robin starting on my right.

Reading Basic Text: We will read 2 paragraphs each.

Reading Sober Dating Focus Booklet: We will read 1 column or 4 paragraphs of the article. After reading, you can share for three minutes or pass.

Answering questions: We will write for 10 minutes on answers to the questions. If you feel you can't relate to any of the questions, write on any of the other questions in the book or on any S.L.A.A. related topic.

After the writing we can share or pass. We will do three-minute shares.

(at the end of the meeting)

I wish to thank those who shared today. Please remember our cherished tradition of anonymity. Who you see here, what you hear here, when you leave here, let it stay here.

After a moment of quiet meditation, will those of you who wish to please join me in the Serenity Prayer?

The Twelve Steps of S.L.A.A.*

1. We admitted we were powerless over sex and love addiction - that our lives had become unmanageable.

2. Came to believe that a Power greater than ourselves could restore us to sanity.

3. Made a decision to turn our will and our lives over to the care of God as we understood God.

4. Made a searching and fearless moral inventory of ourselves.

5. Admitted to God, to ourselves, and to another human being the exact nature of our wrongs.

6. Were entirely ready to have God remove all these defects of character.

7. Humbly asked God to remove our shortcomings.

8. Made a list of all persons we had harmed and became willing to make amends to them all.

9. Made direct amends to such people wherever possible, except when to do so would injure them or others.

10. Continued to take personal inventory and when we were wrong promptly admitted it.

11. Sought through prayer and meditation to improve our conscious contact with a Power greater than ourselves, praying only for knowledge of God's will for us and the power to carry that out.

12. Having had a spiritual awakening as the result of these steps, we tried to carry this message to sex and love addicts, and to practice these principles in all areas of our lives.

The Twelve Traditions of S.L.A.A.*

1. Our common welfare should come first; personal recovery depends upon S.L.A.A. unity.
2. For our group purpose there is but one ultimate authority -- a loving God as this Power may be expressed through our group conscience. Our leaders are but trusted servants; they do not govern.
3. The only requirement for S.L.A.A. membership is a desire to stop living out a pattern of sex and love addiction. Any two or more persons gathered together for mutual aid in recovering from sex and love addiction may call themselves an S.L.A.A. group, provided that as a group they have no other affiliation.
4. Each group should be autonomous except in matters affecting other groups or S.L.A.A. as a whole.
5. Each group has but one primary purpose -- to carry its message to the sex and love addict who still suffers.
6. An S.L.A.A. group or S.L.A.A. as a whole ought never endorse, finance, or lend the S.L.A.A. name to any related facility or outside enterprise, lest problems of money, property, or prestige divert us from our primary purpose.
7. Every S.L.A.A. group ought to be fully self-supporting, declining outside contributions.
8. S.L.A.A. should remain forever nonprofessional, but our service centers may employ special workers.
9. S.L.A.A. as such ought never be organized; but we may create service boards or committees directly responsible to those they serve.
10. S.L.A.A. has no opinion on outside issues; hence the S.L.A.A. name ought never be drawn into public controversy.
11. Our public relations policy is based on attraction rather than promotion; we need always maintain personal anonymity at the level of press, radio, TV, film, and other public media.
We need guard with special care the anonymity of all fellow S.L.A.A. members.
12. Anonymity is the spiritual foundation of all our traditions, ever reminding us to place principles before personalities.

of money, property and prestige divert us from our primary purpose. 7. Every A.A. group ought to be fully self-supporting, declining outside contributions. 8. Alcoholics Anonymous should remain forever nonprofessional, but our service centers may employ special workers. 9. A.A., as such, ought never be organized; but we may create service boards or committees directly responsible to those they serve. 10. Alcoholics Anonymous has no opinion on outside issues; hence the A.A. name ought never be drawn into public controversy. 11. Our public relations policy is based on attraction rather than promotion; we need always maintain personal anonymity at the level of press, radio, and films. 12. Anonymity is the spiritual foundation of all our Traditions, ever reminding us to place principles before personalities.

The Twelve Concepts for World Service of S.L.A.A.*

1. Ultimate responsibility and authority for S.L.A.A. world services always reside in the collective conscience of our whole Fellowship.

2. The Annual Business Conference, by delegation, is the voice and conscience for our world services and of S.L.A.A. as a whole.

3. To insure effective leadership, each element of S.L.A.A. - the Conference, the Board of Trustees, staff, and committees - all possess the "Right of Decision."

4. The "Right of Participation" is maintained by allowing members the opportunity to cast one vote up to the level at which they are trusted servants.

5. The "Right of Appeal" prevails so that minority opinion is heard and personal grievances receive careful consideration.

6. The Conference recognizes that the chief initiative and active responsibility in most world service matters should be exercised by the trustee members of the Conference acting as the Board of Trustees.

7. The Articles of Incorporation and the By-Laws of the Fellowship are legal instruments, empowering the trustees to manage and conduct world service affairs. Although the Conference Charter is a legal document; it also relies on tradition and the power of the S.L.A.A. purse for final effectiveness.

8. The trustees are the principal planners and administrators of overall policy and finance. They have custodial oversight of the separately incorporated and constantly active services, including their ability to hire staff.

9. Good service leaders, together with sound and appropriate methods of choosing them, are at all levels indispensable for our future functioning and safety. The primary world service leadership must be assumed by the Board of Trustees.

10. Every service responsibility is matched by equal service authority – the scope of this authority is always well defined whether by tradition, by resolution, by specific job description or by appropriate charters and by-laws.

11. The trustees need the best possible committees, staff, and consultants. Composition, qualifications, induction procedures, systems of rotation, and rights and duties are always matters of serious concern.

12. The Conference observes the spirit of S.L.A.A. Tradition, a. taking care that it never becomes the seat of perilous wealth or power; b. that sufficient operating funds and reserve be its prudent financial principle; c. that it place none of its members in a position of unqualified authority over others; d. that it reach all important decisions by discussion, vote, and, whenever possible, by substantial unanimity; e. that its actions never be personally punitive nor an incitement to public controversy; f. that it never perform acts of government, and that, like the Fellowship it serves, it will always remain democratic in thought and action.

141

A.A. Twelve Concepts (short form)

1. Final responsibility and ultimate authority for A.A. world services should always reside in the collective conscience of our whole Fellowship. 2. The General Service conference of A.A. has become, for nearly every practical purpose, the active voice and the effective conscience of our whole Society in its world affairs. 3. To insure effective leadership, we should endow each element of A.A.-the Conference, the General Service Board its service corporations, staffs, committees, and executives-with a traditional "Right of Decision." 4. At all responsible levels, we ought to maintain a traditional "Right of Participation," allowing a voting representation in reasonable proportion to the responsibility that each must discharge. 5. Throughout our structure, a traditional "Right of Appeal" ought to prevail, so that minority opinion will be heard and personal grievances receive careful consideration. 6. The Conference recognizes that the chief initiative and active responsibility in most world service matters should be exercised by the trustee members of the Conference acting as the General Service Board. 7. The Charter and Bylaws of the General Service Board are legal instruments, empowering the trustees to manage and conduct world service affairs. The Conference Charter is not a legal document; it relies upon tradition and the A.A. purse for final effectiveness. 8. The trustees are the principal planners and administrators of overall policy and finance. They have custodial oversight of the separately incorporated and constantly active services, exercising this through their ability to elect all the directors of these entities. 9. Good service leadership at all levels is indispensable for our future functioning and safety. Primary world service leadership, once exercised by the founders, must necessarily be assumed by the trustees. 10. Every service responsibility should be matched by an equal service authority, with the scope of such authority well defined. 11. The trustees should always have the best possible committees, corporate service directors, executives, staffs, and consultants. Composition, qualifications, induction procedures, and rights and duties will always be matters of serious concern. 12. The Conference shall observe the spirit of A.A. tradition, taking care that it never becomes the seat of perilous wealth or power; that sufficient operating funds and reserve be its prudent financial principle; that it place none of its members in a position of unqualified authority over others; that it reach all important decisions by discussion, vote, and whenever possible, by substantial unanimity; that its actions never be personally punitive nor an incitement to public controversy; that it never perform acts of government, and that, like the society it serves, it will always remain democratic in thought and action.